The Bent-Knee Time
A Bit for Every Day of the Year

By

Samuel Dickey Gordon
Author of "Quiet Talks on Power," and "Quiet Talks on Prayer"

A Yesterday's World Publishing

Published by A Yesterday's World Publishing
Copyright © 2019 A Yesterday's World Publishing
First impression 2019
ISBN - 978-1-912925-81-0

A WORD AT THE START

These daily bits are meant to be little wedges for the Quiet Corner, to get things started.

A life of victory and power hinges on three things: an Act, a Purpose, and a Habit; an initial act, a rock-rooted purpose, and a daily habit; the *act* of surrender to Jesus as Master of one's person and life, the simple, steady *purpose* in everything to do as he would wish, the daily *habit* of getting a bit of time every day off alone with the Master, with door shut, the Book open, the knee bent, and the will bent afresh.

The daily habit needs much emphasis because it puts new life-blood daily into the act and the purpose. After these other two are fixed in where they belong this is *the hinge* on which the whole life swings.

These little bits are meant to be distinctly secondary to the Book itself. They are simply to start one's thoughts a-going, and to help fit the Book into one's own daily life. The chiefest thing always is the fresh touch face-to-face with Jesus. And he always meets one at *the bent-knee time* to give that fresh touch. You can count on that.

S. D. G

Sunday. Mark 1:1-11.

MAKING A WAY FOR JESUS.

This is *the* thing, to prepare the way for Jesus. John did it. Jesus needed it. He needs it. We can do it. By purity of life, earnestness of purpose, gentleness of spirit we can open the way for Jesus into hearts and homes. We *may;* it is our privilege. We *can;* it is in our power. We *must;* Jesus' love in the heart drives us to it. Surely we *will;* this shall be our glad, set purpose.

Monday. Isa. 40:3-5; Mal. 3:1-6.

FINDING GOD'S PLAN.

Everyone's life is foreplanned. It seems hard for us to take this in as really so. But that's the kind of a God our God is. A simple shepherd lad, years ago, tending sheep, found out that all the plan for his life was written down in a book beforehand, God's own record book, Ps. 139:16. We may find this out, too. God will foretell us his plan. May we not fail God, nor his plan!

Tuesday. Luke 1:8-17.

GOD NEVER FAILS.

God never forgets. He never loses count of prayers nor of time. Prayers may seem unanswered. But, when the heart's in right touch, there's always thoughtful love in the delay. The waiting-time is a training-time for us. More is being planned for by God than had been prayed for by us. Hannah found this out with Samuel, and Zacharias with John. *Let's keep faith's fire burning* even through long waits and heavy rains.

Wednesday. John 1:19-30.

POINTING TO JESUS WITH YOUR LIFE.

John pointed to Jesus. He did it so wholeheartedly that people forgot the pointer, and looked at Jesus. Every question brought a "not" about himself, which emphasized the word about Jesus. The voice spoke so distinctly and self-forgetfully that men were caught only by what was said. Each of us may be *an index-finger pointing to Jesus.* The home-life, the controlling spirit, the daily touch with others, *may* make others think of him.

Thursday. John 3:26-36.

STICKING STEADILY TO IT.

John did the thing he was asked to do. He began, and kept on, and he finished it up. He tied a knot on the end of a thread. It's good to begin; it's better to keep undiscourageably going; it's best to stick it out to the end, regardless of difficulties. Starters are plenty, but stickers are scarce, and finishers are scarcer. Let's stick it out on the thing we are doing for Jesus, prayerfully and singingly.

Friday. Matt. 9:36-10:8.

ON AN ERRAND FOR JESUS.

Praying is the key to every needed thing. When you pray, something happens. The praying puts you into fresh touch with Jesus. You are where you can be used. The praying man is given power. He can be trusted with it. For he will use it only as the Master guides. He can help his fellows in their need most. The closer we keep in prayer with Jesus the more we can help our fellows.

Saturday.

Matt. 11:2-9.

WHEN ITS DARK TRUST MORE.

Trust trusts God when it doesn't understawd what he is doing. John was puzzled. Jesus was filling out the *personal* part of his mission; but not the *official,* the kingly part. The people were being helped. But John, the King's herald, was a prisoner. What did it mean? Was someone else coming to fill out the other part? Jesus practically replies, "Wait; hold steady; trust me, though you don't see how things are working out."

Second Week

Sunday.

Mark 1:12-20.

JESUS IS ALONGSIDE TO HELP.

Jesus touched every side of human life. He did it by giving a bit of his own life. He took a decisive stand in the Jordan with God's messenger. He was tempted. He came into personal friendship with men. He took men into close partnership in his blessed ministry. He revealed the resistless power of God helping human need. And he still does. He will begin this sort of thing in us as we let him.

Monday.

Matt. 3:16-4:11.

A TEMPTATION IS A CHANCE FOR VICTORY.

Jesus was tempted, really tempted. No one was ever tempted so cunningly and repeatedly. The tempter did his best and worst. And Jesus felt the temptations keenly. Many a time his brow was moist and his jaw set. But every temptation met its full match in him. He overcame by his set will and his Father's grace. And so may we, by his victory and his help. Temptation is a chance for victory through Jesus.

Tuesday.

Heb. 4:14-5:9.

A FRIEND IN A TIGHT CORNER.

Jesus was the Brother of man as well as the Son of man. He shared our experiences. He trod the same rough road, and knew the same tight corners. He was tempted as we are. and he was tempted first, and he was tempted most. The path's never so rough for *our* feet. His have smoothed it down. He understands. He *can* help; he knows by experience. And he *will* help, and *we shall have victory today.*

Wednesday.

Isa. 42:1-8.

SPELLING "IDEAL" WITH AN "R."

God carries an ideal in his heart. Eden pictures that ideal most winsomely—God and man walking and working in a garden as closest friends. Sin broke the ideal. God gave his Son to heal the hurt of sin and woo us back to the garden-life. Both prophecy and gospel tell how practical and winsome his wooing was. God'll never rest content till his ideal has become real. Let us make it real today.

Thursday.

John 1:35-47.

KEEPING "IN TOUCH."

Jesus winning five men one after another into personal friendship—how like him and his Father! For God loves the personal touch. When he created man he gave a bit of himself, his breath. When man lost touch he gave his only Son to get us back in touch. And Jesus gave his own very self, his life, in doing it. Let us keep in close, personal touch with Jesus, and help somebody get in touch, too.

Friday.   Luke 5:1-11.

GIVING JESUS A PULPIT.

A boat for a pulpit! Who would have thought it? How glad Peter must have been! Probably he never forgot it. The old boat never seemed quite the same again. But that's a way Jesus has, using our common things in his uncommon task of helping and winning men: patched-up fishing-nets, a carpenter's bench, the curb of an old well, water-jugs. He'll use our kitchen and shop, store and office, to help men today, if he may.

Saturday.   John 2:1-11.

LIMITLESS POWER WAITING AT YOUR FINGER-TIPS.

Jesus fitted his help in just where it was needed. He never used his power to show that he could, but to help somebody. The people were hungry, and he fed them. The widow was broken-hearted over her boy, and Jesus brought him back to life. The tax-collector called, and he helped Peter pay the bill. The wedding supplies ran out, and he renewed them. His power is at hand today to help in the common things of our daily lives.

Third Week

Sunday.   Mark 1:21-34.

LET YOUR HEART CONTROL YOUR HAND.

Jesus couldn't help working. He had a tender heart. He *felt* the need of the crowds. He couldn't withstand the plea of their need. His heart responded. His hand reached out quickly to help. No criticism or scorn or opposition could hold hack the thing so sorely needed. *The work grew out of a heart* in touch with his Father and with the needy crowds. This is the secret of true working. now as then.

Monday.   Mark 1:35-45.

FRESH TOUCH WITH GOD.

Jesus was never too busy to pray. That explains his close, helpful touch with men. That was a busy day in the Galilæan fishing-town. But he was up early the next morning for the fresh talk with the Father; that came first. Out of it grew the clear vision of the next towns with their needs, though it was easier to stay with the enthusiastic Capernaum crowds. Prayer clears the vision, warms the heart, and makes us practical.

Tuesday.   Acts 10:34-43.

LETTING JESUS OUT THROUGH OUR LIVES.

The sun needs no recommendation on a winter's day; nor the steady downpour of rain after a dry spell; *nor Jesus* where there's good to be done, hearts to comfort, sins to forgive, feet to steady, tempted men to be helped. If we can just get folks to know the real Jesus, he'll do all that needs doing. Let us do our best to get men into contact with Jesus. He'll do the rest.

Wednesday.   Luke 4:14-22.

STRONG YIELDING.

It takes strength to yield. The highest act is in yielding to a higher will. Jesus yielded strongly to the control of the Holy Spirit during those human years. And so the Spirit *could* flood his words, and acts, and presence with power. Then the Holy Spirit yielded to Jesus, who sent him down on Pentecost to give *us* power. Let us use our strength in yielding thoughtfully, intelligently, to the Spirit's sway. This is the secret of power.

4

Thursday.   Luke 5:12-16.

HE WILL, TODAY.

Practically, faith is not simply believing that God *can,* but believing that he *will.* That he can do a thing tells of *his power.* And his power has no limit. But there's something immensely more; that's *his love.* His love comes into sympathetic touch with our need; his eye sees; his heart feels; then his hand eagerly stretches out to help. Today Jesus says to each of us. "*I will* do what you need done, if you'll let me."

Friday.   Matt. 11:25-30.

KEEP IN STEP.

"Rest is not quitting earth's busy career;
Rest is the fitting of self to one's sphere."

Keeping step is rest, for the soldier on march, and the man following Jesus. Rhythm of color is beauty. Rhythm of sound is music. Rhythm of action is power. Jesus made peace by his blood and *gives* it to us. As we keep step with him, we *find* peace stealing softly in, and others find power breathing out. Let's keep in step with Jesus.

Saturday.   Ps. 103:1-3.

PRAISE OPENS THE SKYLIGHT.

You can't remember all, but be sure you don't *forget* all. Praise opens the door wider for more. Thanksgiving clears the skies and quickens your step. Doing your daily, common task to the sound of music—some song with Jesus' name in—lightens the work, strengthens both heart and arm, gets more work done and better, brightens the day, helps your neighbor, and gladdens God. Let's sing more. Everything we have is red-marked with Jesus' love.

Fourth Week

Sunday.   Mark 2:1-12.

GOD IN HUMAN SHOES.

Jesus was God coming amongst us in human shoes, to do what needed doing. The sorest need is heart-deep—the sin forgiven, the stain washed out, the power of sin broken, the conscience set free; then the heart full of glad song, and the hands and feet impelled to carry the glad news to others. So he touched the secret springs that control the whole life. It cost his life. But he never flinched. Blessed Jesus!

Monday.   Psalm 32.

HEART-MUSIC.

A heart at peace with God and itself—this is the greatest of blessings. The sin washed out and burned out and the heart kept clean means sweetest music within. Then all the powers, bodily and mental and of the spirit, key up to their best, the mind is open to be taught, the will ready to be guided and shaped, and the telling of the God-story to others is simple and clear and natural and unbroken.

Tuesday.   Luke 15:11-24.

LOVE NEVER FAILS.

Prodigals are thicker than we think. A child dissatisfied with the Father's way, getting all he can for himself, dead-bent on his own way, cutting loose from restraint, clearly a prodigal in spirit, though not at his rope's end—the last stage. But the Father's love clean outdoes any prodigal wilfulness—wise, patient waiting till the dead-end of the blind alley's

5

reached, tireless watching, eager running, the tender embrace, the welcome back. Love outruns the prodigal still.

Wednesday.   Luke 7:41-50.

SEEING THROUGH GOD'S EYES.

Not that you must sin much to be forgiven much and so love much—not that. God doesn't need bad to bring out his good. But when we see how much of a sin one sin is, and how bad a break just one break makes, then we begin to know what love God's love is. Then our hearts are broken that we treated God so, and we're down on our knees in untellable gratitude and eager service. It's worthwhile to see as God sees.

Thursday.   1 John 1.

THE GREATEST THING—A PURE HEART!

It's a great thing to be forgiven—to be back in the old seat by the hearth-fire, the old score wiped off the slate, the heavy heart lightened, the Father smiling gently into your eyes. But there's something more and yet better—to be cleaned up inside; the bad taken out, washed out, and burned out, and a new clean inside put in you. Jesus does both, though it cost him his life to do it.

Friday.   Isa. 1:2-6, 16-18.

THE CHEMISTRY OF LOVE.

We've heard much of late in college about the new chemistry. Do you know about the old chemistry, the oldest, the chemistry of love, God's love? It puts the bright, running red of the blood of Jesus over the dirty black of our sin. And the startling result is a white, a pure, clear white, that neither fades nor yellows. Expensive chemistry that! Sin is awfully expensive. But love stops at nothing to get us clean again.

Saturday.   1 Pet. 1:13-23.

KEEP THE JESUS FIRES BURNING.

When it gets hold of us what Jesus did for us in (lying, everything changes inside and out. We want to be pure for his sake; it cost him so much to clean us up. A passion burns to tell somebody else about him, to do something to open the way for that telling where the door is shut. We *must* serve; it is our life. We *can* serve; we've learned how. For only love service is real service.

Fifth Week

Sunday.   Mark 2:23-3:5.

THE ZEST OF VICTORY.

The old Sabbath was a *rest* day. It came at the end of the week's work. Its observance was a recognition of the love that gave us life and time, strength to work, and enjoyment in rest. The new Sabbath is more—a *victory* day. It tells of Jesus' victory over sin and death. It comes at the beginning of the week's work. So we *start the week with a song* that lasts till Saturday night.

Monday.   Luke 4:16-22.

HOW GOOD GOD IS!

"Worship" grows out of "worth." It really means thinking deep down in your heart how worthy God is; how full of power in making the world so beautiful, and in sustaining life so

6

constantly, even in those who leave him out; how full of love in giving his only Son to die; how patient, and gentle, and winsome, and motherly. It's blessed to do it in the church service. It's yet more blessed to do it in between times.

Tuesday.   Luke 13:10-17.

LIVING MUSICALLY.

When you've learned the real Sabbath song, everything is changed by it. It is the rest song. the rest that comes out of victory. Jesus' victory gives rest of heart. Then we're keeping Sabbath day in our hearts every day. The music of it makes the wheels of life go easier. There's an eagerness to get the Sabbath spirit—the rest spirit—into everybody else, easing pain of body and circumstance and heart for them.

Wednesday.   Isa. 58:6-14.

KEEP THE SABBATH DOOR OPEN.

God. asks a seventh of our time as an acknowledgment that it's *all* his. Giving him the seventh of our time weekly helps bring us into that touch of life where he can flood his best into *all* the days. If we reckon the day as his, in grateful acknowledgment of all he's given us, he will help us steer a wise course between the Sabbath looseness so common, and the old straight-laced rigor that made the day a burden.

Thursday.   Exod. 16:21-30.

THOUGHTFUL PREPAREDNESS.

Thinking ahead is common with thoughtful people. The housewife "sets the sponge" the night before. The engineer "oils up" before train-time. Even the squirrel stores away nuts for winter, and the dog'll bury a bone against hungry-time. Nothing ever *happens:* whatever good comes has been thought out by somebody. *Let us plan ahead thoughtfully, sensibly, for God's day.* It'll make the day more restful and sweeter, and put a hallowing touch on all the weekdays, too.

Friday.   Mark 16:1-9.

THE REAL SABBATH FRAGRANCE.

Jesus rose on "the first day of the week." We can never forget that. That alone would make it the *first* of all days for us. The women brought the fragrant spices, but they didn't use them. A richer, subtler fragrance had already been breathed into the day. The early disciples never forgot the day nor its fragrance. And we later disciples will do well to remember weekly *the sweet odor of that great first day.*

Saturday.   Rev. 1:9-20.

THE BIT OF QUIET TIME.

John was far from home and loved ones. Ile must have felt the loneliness of it. Was he depressed? It wouldn't have been surprising. But when the Lord's Day came he had a bit of quiet time alone with the Master. And the gracious Spirit came a bit closer, brooding like a mother. And then came the wondrous vision of the glorified Christ. Let us, too, he in the Spirit on the Lord's Day. It'll bring Christ closer to us.

Sixth Week

Sunday.   Mark 3:13-19.

HAVE YOU VOLUNTEERED?

Jesus is looking for men. He needs men. He uses men. He chooses the men he uses. *The* qualification he looks for is willingness, strong, earnest. intelligent willingness, to do what he wants done. He takes such men into habitual companionship with himself. So they catch fire with his passion, learn his purpose and plans, are filled with his power, know the music of his peace, and gladly sacrifice, if need be. *May we not fail Jesus!*

Monday. Luke 6:12-16.

KNEE POWER FOR THE DAILY JOB.

He picked them out on his knees. Slowly, thoughtfully, through the night, he sifted back and forth, taking account of weaknesses and drawbacks, till at last the list of twelve men stood clear. A great night's work, that, getting fishermen ready to be apostles. No wonder Peter came back, and John's fire burned out in love. That night's knee work did it. Nothing human can resist quiet, steady, confident knee work. *Try it on your daily job.*

Tuesday. John 15:15-27.

PIPE-LINE PARTNERS.

The Holy Spirit would bear witness of Jesus. "And ye *also* shall bear witness," Jesus said. They added their bit. They could do nothing without the Holy Spirit. And, reverently let us say it, the Spirit could not do his work without them. They must let him use them as he needed. They became the pipe-line through which the water of life flowed. Are you an *"also"? Are you adding your bit*—your life? It is needed. That's the plan.

Wednesday. Luke 14:25-35.

FOOTING THE BILLS.

Everything worthwhile costs. And you can tell its worth by how much it cost—some-body. It cost God much to give his only Son. It cost Jesus both reputation and life to save us. He saved others, but he couldn't save himself from the awful cost of saving us. It costs to sin. Selfishness is awfully costly. And it costs to follow Jesus. really, truly, fully. But *it's worth all it costs,* and immensely more.

Thursday. John 17:9-21.

JESUS IS PRAYING MOST NOW.

Jesus is still praying. He ever lives to pray us through. Thirty years of living, three years of serving, one tremendous act of dying, nineteen hundred years of praying! What an emphasis on prayer! Yet all through, praying had its roots deep down in the living, and serving, and dying. And the prayer at heart is this: that *love,* real love, *might flood our lives,* purifying, unifying, and perfecting. Let us pray and—love.

Friday. Matt. 10:14-25.

THAT KNOTTED PLACE.

Jesus is Master: we are disciples. He leads: we follow where he leads. The path is a plain one to eyes that keep close to him. The prints of his feet may be clearly seen, often red-marked. His hand reaches out to take ours. *There's a little knotted place in the palm of his.* That grips our hearts greatly as we follow. And his voice may be clearly heard by ears trained in the quiet corner with the Book.

Saturday. Matt. 19:23-30.

THE HIGHEST REWARD.

Partners with Jesus—daily, friendly touch with himself, being taken into his confidence, knowing something of his plans, being sent on errands for him, hearing his quiet voice of approval—could there be greater, sweeter reward than just this? Yet there is. There will be need of trained, trusty workers in the coming Kingdom-time. Those who have learned how, even a little, now, will be the trusted ones then. Yet *we'll be thinking more of the Master than of the reward.*

Seventh Week

Sunday.   Mark 4:1-8. 14-20.

LIVE IT!

Jesus taught. But he lived what he taught. And he lived it *first* before he taught it. And he lived it *most,* more than *even he* ever could teach it. On the human side here was the great power of his teaching. He will teach us. We need it. We need it daily. But *we must live it as we learn it;* then we can teach it to others. This is the first rule in Jesus' school.

Monday.   Gal. 5:16-24.

WHO'S IN THE LEAD?

There are two leaders. Everyone is walking behind one or the other. The evil leader covers up so we shan't suspect whom we're walking behind. But the things he leads you to do are a sure telltale mark—selfish, passionate, sinful things. The other leader is as open as the things he leads you to do are good. An unselfish love welling up inside controls heart, and tongue, and head. *Today's life tells whom you arc walking behind.*

Tuesday.   Luke 21:29-36.

DON'T GET DIZZY.

To be drunk means you've taken so much of *something* that you've lost control. You may get drink-drunk, food-drunk, pleasure-drunk, or anxiety-drunk. The word rendered "surfeiting" really means to get dizzy. The only safe rule on liquor is total abstinence; and on other things this: don't get dizzy; never lose control of heart, or head, or tongue, or hand. *Live each day so you'll be glad to see Jesus whenever he comes back.*

Wednesday.   Eph. 5:11-21.

KEEP ON TOP.

Evil insists on pushing its way in. Sometimes it's very subtle and snaky. There are three things you can do: Yield to it; that's bad. Play with it; don't say no to it, but don't oppose it; that's bad, too, but very common. *The only right thing is to be aggressively good* and Jesus-like, in a tactful way; then you'll overcome it. Be not overcome of evil, nor play with it, but overcome it.

Thursday.   Prov. 23:29-35.

KEEP THE ENEMY CLEAN OUT.

There's only one safe thing to do with alcoholics of every grade and kind: treat them as you would a poisonous snake. You never know when they'll bite. Never take the *first* drink. or if you have, never take the *next* one. *Drinking is like giving the front-door key to a burglar.* Everything inside is in danger when the first glass is taken; nothing is quite safe— brain, tongue, heart, purity, character, loved ones, property.

Friday.   Dan. 1:8-16.

FIRST THINGS IN FIRST PLACE.

Loyalty means being true. Principle means the first thing. Be true to first things—purity of heart and body, honesty of word and life, obedience to God, unselfish love toward all. Never waver on these for a moment, by so much as the half-breadth of a narrow hair. *Keep first things in first place* and other things'll take care of themselves. There's nothing so manly and womanly as being true, and nothing so Christly as being gentle.

Saturday.   1 Cor. 6:9-11, 19, 20.

STAY UP.

Don't lower yourself to sin. Sin is *down,* low down, mean, and base. We belong *up.* God made us *up* on his own level. The Holy Spirit lives in us, in our very bodies, to bring us *up* and keep us *up.* Honor your body. A lie, a foul word, an unclean thought or mental picture or act, a dishonest word or look or act—these lower us and dishonor him who lives in us. *Don't lower yourself.*

Eighth Week

Sunday.   Mark 4:21-34.

THE GROWING-PLACE.

Where Jesus' touch is allowed full sway we shall grow. Little by little, day by day, pushing off the old, pushing out the new, becoming more and better: more victory in temptation, more purity in life, more patience with others, more knowledge of his will through the Book, more getting things done through prayer, more winsomeness in winning. But we'll not be *continually* measuring *how much*—sometimes; we'll just be *staying in the sunlight and dew of Jesus' presence.*

Monday.   Zech. 4:1-14.

WHEN LITTLE IS BIG.

The day of small things can become the life of biggest and best things. A small word spoken at the right time may set a whole life straight. A gentle smile may brighten the way for the man with a heavy load. The small bit of time with the Book and the knee bent will hallow the day's task. The still, small voice listened to may turn the world's tide. *The small in God's hand becomes big.*

Tuesday.   Luke 2:40-52.

KEEP OPEN TO THE BEST.

Jesus was natural in boyhood as he was in manhood. He ate, and slept, and worked. He companioned with others, read in the Bible he had, aimed to live it out, got alone on his knees, obeyed his mother, dreamed of the future. *he kept open to the best*—body, mind, spirit—in a simple boy-way. So he grew. So we, too, shall grow in vigor and gentleness and strength of life, as he has sway.

Wednesday.   1 Pet. 2:1-5; 2 Pet. 3:14-18.

GARDENS AND GARDENERS.

The Bible is a garden book. There's one at the beginning, a better one at the end, and the Gethsemane garden in between. Every man should be a gardener, and his life the garden. There's sowing and sunshine, dew-fall and rain, and special watering in dry spells. Then there's weeding, watching for hurtful insects, and pruning, a cutting back to get better fruit. *Let's be good gardeners,* with the Man of Gethsemane to help.

Thursday.   Matt. 13:24-30.

RIVAL GARDENERS.

Evil, like weeds, grows rank and fast without cultivation, we *think.* But it isn't so.

There's another gardener, a special, unseen gardener for evil. He sows, and waters, and cultivates, and tries to weed out the good. He's an old hand at gardening. He stays up nights, watching for chances. We must fight him. The best way is to get our crop in *first;* weed and work it sleeplessly. *The best work in this garden is done down on your knees.*

Friday.   Isa. 61:1-11.

A GARDEN OF EDEN YET.

What a race it is between weeds and insects and woody, leafy growths *and* big, juicy fruitage! It's so in gardens, and in the garden of your life, and in the garden of the world. It looks sometimes as if the weeds were "taking" the world garden. But it's not so. *The Chief Gardener'll clean up the weeds some day,* and then the garden will have a good chance. And the yield will satisfy the hunger of all men.

Saturday.   Acts 2:37-47.

THY KINGDOM COME QUICKLY.

The Kingdom will come some day with the coming of the King. Then the other prince, the pretender prince of this world, will go. God's will of love and purity will be done down on this old earth, even as up in the heavens. And the other will of bitterness and selfishness and hate will be undone. And the old world will know *the sweetness and beauty of God's early Eden ideal.* "Thy kingdom come." It's pretty badly needed.

Ninth Week

Sunday.   Mark 4:35-41.

KEEPING IN TUNE.

Rhythm of sound is music. Rhythm of color is beauty. Rhythm of action is peace and power. Peace within, deep as the sea, still as the stars, fragrant as locust blossoms in May, as undisturbable as the everlasting hills. Jesus made peace by the Cross. We find peace as we stay in full rhythmic touch with him. *Let's keep in step with Jesus.* Then we shall know the inner music of peace, and others will feel the fragrant touch of power.

Monday.   Mark 5:1-15.

THE MASTER MUSICIAN.

When Jesus takes command he brings peace. The storms must cease—storms of passion and temper. The prisoner is set free. His chains are broken—chains of selfishness and anxiety. Jesus' clear voice rings out, "Peace, be still," and there's a great calm. Like the sweet cadences of music runs the phrase through the Book, "fear not." *Let us put Jesus in command,* and obey him fully, and we shall know an inner quiet, greater even than the word "peace" expresses.

Tuesday.   Ps. 147:1-5, 14-18.

BRINGING THE MASTER BACK.

Whenever our Lord Jesus comes back, there'll he peace in the world's borders, and not before. "He maketh wars to cease." The hurt of the earth will be healed. The tangle of the world will be smoothed out. The bitterness and bickerings will stop, and the hot fires of hate and self-seeking be put out. The earth will yield unprecedented harvests. *We can hasten the glad day* by letting him reign in our lives in today's common round.

Wednesday.   Mark 7:31-37.

THE JESUS MUSIC.

Some things can't be hid. Jesus couldn't be. Music can't. The sweet peace of God in the heart can't be hushed up. The face tells it—the quiet eye, the glad smile, the gentle word. The step has a spring to it. The hand does its work differently. And those we're touching know it, too. Sometimes it irritates them; the inner smothered conscience hurts. This is *the chiefest plan for winning men* to Jesus—having his peace rule our hearts.

Thursday.   Phil. 4:4-9.

HEART SOVEREIGNTY.

God's peace "passeth understanding," but it does not pass appreciation. It's too deep for our brains, but not for our hearts. It can't be analyzed and explained, but it can be accepted, and yielded to, and enjoyed. You don't get it; it gets you. It does sentinel duty over your thoughts and imaginations, keeping worry out and trust and obedience in. Paul's threefold rule of peace is simple: *Worry about nothing; pray about everything; be thankful for anything.*

Friday.   Jer. 6:11-16.

OBEDIENCE MEANS RHYTHM.

When the heart's wrong, there *can't* be peace. Selfishness is a gangrene, eating at the very vitals. Sin is a cancer, poisoning the blood. *Peace is the rhythm of our wills with Jesus' love-will.* Disobedience breaks the music. Failure to keep in touch makes discord. The notes jar and grate. We have broken off. The peace can't get in. Jesus made peace by his blood. We get it only by keeping in full .touch with him.

Saturday.   Isa. 9:1-7.

BLESSED TELLTALES.

You can tell Jesus' reign by the Jesus traits. Gloom gives way to gladness. Darkness runs before the flood of light. The drawn face, white and tear-wet, becomes round with joyous smiles. Freedom displaces oppression. Weapons of strife make a good fire to warm by. It'll be true, really, some day, on this old, sin-stained, hurt earth when Jesus does return. It'll be true today in our hearts and circumstances if Jesus is in control.

Tenth Week

Sunday.   Mark 5:21-23, 35-43.

FRESH SUPPLIES.

The sore hurt of sin is everywhere, though it's often hard to trace connections. It robs the body of vigor, the mind of peace and poise, the heart of purity, the life of purpose. *Jesus is ever on the heels of sin, restoring what has been lost.* He re-stores till the overflow reaches others. Vet it took his own life to do it. And it takes our lives, gladly yielded, to get all that he gives.

Monday.   Luke 7:11-18.

THE TIGHT CORNER JESUS' OPPORTUNITY.

Things were at their worst here. A woman had lost her life-friend. Yet she had a son left; only one; more precious because just one. Then he slips from her clinging grasp! She is utterly alone. Her heart is bleeding itself out through her eyes. Things are desperate. But *man's tightest pinch gives Jesus' love its best chance.* And the worst is turned into the best.

12

That's Jesus' way—then, *and still.*

Tuesday. John 11:35-45.

GOD'S BEST OUTDOES SIN'S WORST.

Can a thing be worse than the worst? You're pretty apt to think so when it touches *you.* The "only daughter" had just died—humanly a hopeless case. The "only son" was being carried to his burial—one step further in hopelessness. This "only brother" has been buried four days—the very last degree of hopelessness. But *Jesus' restoring power is unfailing.* And his love is greater yet. He can, and he will, if he may get our consent.

Wednesday. John 5:24-29, 39, 40.

LIFE IS SOMEONE LIVING IN YOU.

Anyone may accept Jesus as a Saviour to be trusted, a Friend to be companioned with, a Master to be obeyed. Then he comes in. And with him conies life—purity of heart, victory over temptation, vigor of body, keenness of mind, patience under difficulties, guidance in perplexities, loving sympathy with others, faithfulness in common things. *The* thing is to let Jesus *in* habitually. There will he as much of life as there is of him in the life.

Thursday. John 10:10-18.

TO–FOR–WITH.

The oriental shepherd *gives himself* to his sheep. He shares their life. He eats with them, sleeps with them, braves the storm with them, plans for them, guides them continually, and tights their enemies as his own. He *loves* them. If need be, he gives his life to save theirs. This is what Jesus does. He gave himself *for* us on Calvary. And *he gives himself to us in the daily need of our lives*

Friday. Acts 3:11-19.

THE QUALITY OF LIFE.

The Prince of life *gives* life. He *is* life. He controls it. He restores it when lost. He came to give it—more plentifully, and the better sort. "Eternal life" doesn't mean simply *length.* "Eternal" isn't a foot-rule word. It means *the kind. Jesus gives us a purer, stronger, better quality of life now,* in our bodies, and in our daily experiences. Letting him have habitual control is the sanest thing we can do.

Saturday. John 3:1-16.

JESUS' OTHER SELF.

The Holy Spirit is Jesus' other self. He does *in* us what Jesus did *for* us. The longing for purity, the impulse to pray, the light that breaks in on the Book as you read, and on your daily questions, the new strength that comes—these tell of the Spirit's presence within. As we yield habitually and gladly to Jesus, *the Spirit within has a freer hand,* and so his presence means life.

Eleventh Week

Sunday. Mark 6:7-13, 30.

WITH A GLAD RESPONSE.

Jesus draws and drives. He draws us irresistibly to himself. His peace sings its soft music within. His love kindles fires on the hearthstone of the heart. So he drives us out; not *from* him. *for* him, out to others, nearest and farthest. For love serves. It gives freely. It goes gladly. It sacrifices without thinking of the word. It must serve; that is its life. It can serve; for *only love-service is real service.*

Monday.   Luke 5:1-11.
THERE'S A FIRE.
We catch the spirit of him who saves us. That's a serving spirit. Yet we're not thinking of it as service, nor counting up how much we've done. We're thinking of him who did so much for us. *Love for Jesus becomes a fire in our bones,* and we arc thinking about how to get Jim and Dick and Mary and the rest of them to know him. We'll do lots of things for others, to have them get to know him.

Tuesday.   Matt. 28:16-20.
I CAN DO IT.
When Jesus asks us to do a thing he always gives us power to do it. We often feel that we can't. The call seems clear enough. The thing ought to be done. Yet there's such a strong feeling of inability. But—let's remember, *whom God calls, he qualifies.* When he sends, he gives power to go. As we obey, the power comes, stealing gently, irresistibly in and out. The commission includes all you need.

Wednesday.   Acts 1:6-8; 2:1-4.
PERSONAL FRAGRANCE.
Someone comes in when the door swings wide to Jesus. We call that someone the "Holy Spirit." He kindles a soft but intense fire inside. You find yourself instinctively doing things for others, and telling them of Jesus. And as you do there's a something—a gentle, winsome, burning something—that wings its way into people's hearts like morning sunlight into a room. The word used for it is "power." But the thing is more than the word ever tells.

Thursday.   Rom. 10:6-15.
MOVING IN BY GETTING OUT.
Jesus let all the way in, and then let all the way out—that's the message for all the world. His blood cleanses. his presence changes heart and habits. Then he pushes his way out through the new light in the eye, the new gentleness of the tongue, the new earnestness of the life, out through word and gold and ready feet. His coming in brings life. *His getting out makes you know better that he's in.*

Friday.   Luke 14:16-24.
CAN HE COUNT ON ME?
"Faithful" doesn't mean being full of faith, though a faithful man is. It means that others can count on you. It means sticking to the thing you have been given to do, regardless of criticism, or ridicule, or indifference, or opposition. Jesus was faithful. His Father could count on him. So can we. He may count on us that, by his help, *we'll stick to the thing he's given us to do.* Let's change that "may" to a "can."

Saturday.   Ps. 96:1-13.
THE OUT-GO MEASURES THE IN-COME.
You can tell how much of Jesus has gotten into a man by how much Jesus gets out through the man. You know how far in he's gotten by how far out he's getting. *There's just as much of Jesus in as gets out.* The Jesus-life grows more only by spending itself out. Let's let Jesus all the way in; then he can get all the way out to all the world that he died for.

Twelfth Week

Sunday.   Mark 6:32-44.

THE RESISTLESS MAGNET.

The crowds drew Jesus down from his Father's house, into close touch with their sore need. Into keenest suffering and sacrifice for their sakes, they drew him. *Men's need tugged constantly at Jesus' great heart.* Whatever thing they needed he gave, and gave it freely, yet always thoughtfully. He came not to get but to give. And he still gives as men need. And so does the Jesus-man, as the Spirit guides. It's a sure mark.

Monday.   Mark 10:35-45.

THE GET-SPIRIT.

Most men spend most of their waking hours *getting*. So they provide bread and bed. But if this necessity gets into control, the spirit of a man's life is getting. That means a dead sea. Every stream turns in. He may give; and yet the *get-spirit* be in control. Jesus, too. spent most of his human years getting, earning a livelihood; but the controlling spirit was to give, even to his life. We may be like him.

Tuesday.   Exod. 16:14-24.

FROM HAND TO MOUTH.

Nobody likes to live from hand to mouth; it seems beggarly. These wilderness folk did. They couldn't help themselves. There was no other way. When you sift down into the thing, so do *we!* Yes, we all live literally from hand to mouth. But then *it's God's hand to our months.* If God cut us off for one day, where should we be! Think into it a bit. How grateful we should be for such a faithful God!

Wednesday.   John 6:27-39.

THE PIERCED HAND.

Jesus is God giving us everything we need. His creative hand gives life itself, and food, clothing, shelter, loved ones, and home for enjoying life. His pierced hand gives a clean heart, an obedient spirit, bodily health, a strong purpose, and glad service for our fellows. No one can live without bread. And *no one lives really to the full without Jesus,* taken into his daily life as truly as food is taken into his body.

Thursday.   1 John 3:14-24.

THE "DO" CREED.

We really believe just as much as we *do;* the rest is religious talk. We're saved by faith in Jesus. And the real, simple article of faith, in good working order, controls the habits and hand and purse. Most of our brothers of all the world today are hungry, actually; and yet hungrier for the Bread of life. And we have it. And we can give it. Are we? Or, are we keeping most for ourselves?

Friday.   Matt. 25:31-40.

THE REAL THING.

Religion, the real thing, is so intensely practical. Jesus fed people. He healed their sick. He helped pay bills due. He told them when they were wrong, gently but plainly. He helped them just where they were. What he *did* was so much more than what he said. And so it will be with the Jesus-swayed man. He can't help it. What he is and does clean outweighs what he says. *How much real religion have you and I?*

Saturday.   Matt. 25:14-23.

OUR LEVEL HEST.

We have nothing to do with how much ability we've got, or how little, but with what
we do with what we have. The man with great talent is apt to be puffed up, and the man
with little to belittle the little. Poor fools: God gives it, much or little. *Our part is to lie
faithful.* doing the level best with every bit and scrap. And we will be if Jesus' spirit
controls.

Thirteenth Week

Sunday.   Phil. 2:1-11.

HE'LL HELP US REACH IT.

Imitating is the commonest act of life. Everything depends on whom and what we
imitate. An example, true and winsome—this is *the* need. Jesus was just this. In his
simplicity, his unselfishness, his purity, his earnestness, his devotion to his Father, his
sympathy for men, he is *the* Example. Then he's more; he gives power to follow the Example. *Keep your eye on Jesus.*

Monday.   Matt. 3:13-17; 4:12-16.

STEADY! STEADY THERE!!

Jesus started in on the great task appointed him. It was uphill work from the start. There
seemed no chance, humanly, of getting through. There was every chance, humanly, of
failing dismally. But he had no doubt of the Father's plan; that was enough. Steadily,
prayerfully, he began. The first step was clear. He took it, and took it heel and toe, fully and
bravely. *This is the way for us.* He's our Example.

Tuesday.   Mark 2:13-22.

THE HUMANNESS OF REAL LOVE.

Jesus had principles. but no hard-and-fast rules. He never wavered a jot on principle.
But he was *as pliable as love* when it came to fitting into people's needs. He met people
where they were. He gave them just what they needed, forgiving sins, or giving bread for
their hunger. With greatest patience and thoughtfulness he adapted himself so as to help and
win. It's the love-rule of service. He's our Example.

Wednesday.   Luke 6:12-19.

PATIENCE-LOVE AT ITS BEST.

Jesus let others help him. We may think *He* could have gotten along without help, if anybody
could or can. They weren't the best helpers. They stumbled, and blundered, and—worse. They
didn't understand him. They misunderstood him, and they hindered him, too. It would have been
easier without them, sometimes. But patiently, gently, without getting provoked, he let them help
him. It was a great thing for them. And he's our Example in service.

Thursday.   Man. 13:18-23, 31, 32.

NEVER LOSE HEART.

All sorts of folk to work with: some locked up to your approaches; some unappreciative
of the best you do; some utterly indifferent; some *seeming* hopeful, then proving so un-
steady and wobbly. But *difficulties only show the great need.* They couldn't stop Jesus, nor
take the edge off his eager gentleness. Love grew in its hold. Little by little, more and more,
it grew. This is the Jesus-way.. And he's our Example in service.

16

Friday. Mark 5:25-34.

THE ACID TEST OF SERVICE.

Jesus really helped folks. They were different when he'd touched them. This is the acid test of service. Statistics are good, and up-to-date methods, and bigger attendance, and all that—all good. But *the* thing is this: Are people helped? Is there more peace in the heart? less selfishness in the life? more love in the home? more answered prayer? more real life? It was always so with Jesus. And his way is the way for us.

Saturday. Mark 6:53-56.

THE JESUS-FIRE IN THE HEART.

Love keeps moving out to help someone. Gently as the dewfall, resistlessly as the sun-light, regardless of obstacles as a glacier in the Alps, it keeps reaching out. Difficulties lure it on. Do *you* know about this? If you know Jesus you do. Love sent him down to our earth. His love in the heart sends you out joyously, tirelessly, winsomely, to help someone else. For *Jesus is a fire in the heart* as well as the Example.

Fourteenth Week

Sunday. Mark 7:1-13.

SIN'S KNOTS.

Sin tics a man up, hands and feet, head and heart, and puts on hard knots. If it can't do it directly, then indirectly. If it can't do it fully, it gets all it can. If straight-out sin can't get hold, selfishness usually can, and tight hold, too. And custom, prejudice, habit, superstition—these tie a man up. It's a pretty safe guess that *every one of us is a slave to something*. What is it with *you?*

Monday. Mark 7:24-30.

TIED UP OR FREE?

Jesus undoes sin's work. He unties sin's knots, tears away the bonds, sets the man free, and flushes in new life. Sin cripples the body with weakness and disease, the mind with stupidity and prejudice, the spirit with selfishness and self-will, and the life with stain and evil habit. When Jesus is allowed free swing he frees body, mind, spirit, and life of all that hurts, and gives new life in flood-tide measure.

Tuesday. Mark 7:31-37.

JESUS HEALS.

Jesus healed men of their bodily ailments when he was down here. And he still does. He uses and blesses human knowledge and skill, and he heals also, by direct touch. Yet frequently he permits ailments to remain unhealed so that we may be healed of our stubborn ways, and be wrought into sweet, full accord with himself. Satan contests this ground stubbornly. He imitates God's healing. *Jesus gladly heals when he can have full sway in the life.*

Wednesday. Gal. 5:1-13.

WHAT JESUS DID.

The commonest belief everywhere, Christendom and heathendom alike, is that we earn salvation by what we do. The fear of not being able to pull through haunts men. *Yet we're saved only by what Jesus has done.* He frees us from this haunting fear. We're free to serve for love's sake. And he fills our hearts with the love that makes us gentle and patient with all whom we touch, regardless of what they think or say.

Thursday.   1 Thess. 5:14-24.

THE ZEST OF BEING FREE.

When your lungs are full of fresh air, how stale a shut-up room smells! When a man's free of actual slavery, how irksome its bonds seem to him! *The sheer delight of freedom can't be told.* So when once a man is free of other kinds of slavery—bad habits, lack of self-control, worrying, and that whole brood, what a sweet sense of freedom! Do *you* know about this? You may, today, if Jesus may have his way.

Friday.   Rom. 6:14-23.

SIN'S STINGER.

Sin's a hard master. It snaps a long whip with a stinger on the end. It exacts slavish obedience. Jesus breaks sin's hold. He cuts off that stinger, and breaks the whip. He asks obedience, too, but how different. Obedience is really a music word. It's *the rhythm of your will, at its strongest, with Jesus' will.* Obedience is best when you're not thinking so much about obeying, but about pleasing your Friend.

Saturday.   John 8:30-39.

CHAINED FREEDOM.

Here is *a three-linked chain that sets free*—"abide," "disciples," "know the truth." "Abide"—that's keeping in touch with Jesus. "Disciples"—that's listening with open mind. "Know the truth"—that's experiencing its power in the actual daily round of things. The result—freedom of body from weakness, of mind from immaturity and prejudice, of spirit from worry and bitterness, of life from any touch of sin and selfishness. Do *you* know the liberty of this chain?

Fifteenth Week

Sunday.   Mark 8:27-38.

BE TRUE WHEN IT'S HARD.

Jesus was true to us when he was down here. Vet it wasn't easy. Being true was never harder. It drove him clear to Calvary's shame. But he went. He never flinched. And he never fails us now. No matter how we have been untrue, or neglectful, or ashamed, or have ignored him, when we come, sorry, for help, he always gives it. Surely we'll be true to him in speech and life, no matter how hard!

Monday.   Mark 8:1-13.

JESUS'LL NEVER FAIL YOU.

Jesus gives before he asks. He gives more than he asks. He thinks into our need, of body, and life, and purse. He puts all his power at our command. He promises to fill full every lack of ours. *He'll do an act of creation before he'll let his word fail* any needing, trusting follower. Then he asks that we shall be as loyal to him under every circumstance as he is to us.

Tuesday.   Mark 8:14-26.

CAN YOU HEAR?

What a thoughtful, wise Friend Jesus is! He gladly hears our prayer for bread and bed, shelter of roof, and strength of body. But he's always reaching through these things to the higher, deeper, better things, teaching our minds, and wooing our hearts. *There's a voice speaking to us in the common things* we receive today. He's the wise man who hears and opens up his heart and life for the better things.

18

Wednesday.   1 Kings 18:30-39.
DON'T DROP YOUR FLAG.
The test must come. And it does. Every day brings it anew. A man must line up and show his colors. Satan is aggressive. Sin forces the issue. Selfishness knocks loud at the door daily. They push in, and demand space and recognition, and get it, too. *Jesus earnestly asks that we be true to him.* We should let the colors fly in home, and shop, and school, tactfully, graciously, but unmistakably.

Thursday.   Ps. 63:1-11.
THE FRESH HEART TOUCH.
When a man has a heart-to-heart talk alone *with* God daily, he's pretty apt to talk, with both life and lip, in the crowd *for* God. Keep the inner heart touch with God fresh, and the outer touches are sure to be true and winsome. The outer hinges on the inner. Your prayer-contacts control your contact with your fellows, and with commonplace things. *The knees decide the language of the lips.*

Friday.   Luke 9:57-62.
A RULE WITH NO EXCEPTIONS.
The "Follow Me" road has some rough places. Sin made the road rough for Jesus' feet, and makes it rough for all who follow. Though it is never so rough now since his pierced feet have trodden it. Still, quite rough enough. The rule of the road is simple but radical and never to be changed: *"Put Jesus first."* Then the touch of his presence will make you forget the roughness of the road, even while your feet feel it.

Saturday.   Matt. 10:32-39.
DON'T STRADDLE.
Whenever the issue is distinctly drawn, then always line up with Jesus, winsomely, steadily, decidedly, unmistakably. This is what "confessing" means. In home and shop, in social gathering and church, even though your dearest loved ones and friends and acquaintances stay on the other side of that line, or straddle it, yet *you get and stay over on the Jesus side.* And when in doubt—give Jesus the benefit of the doubt.

Sixteenth Week

Sunday.   Mark 9:2-10.
THE STEADYING LOOK.
Jesus was thinking of the sore test ahead for his disciples when he would go to the cross. So now he quietly drew aside the garment of his humanity and let the God within look out into their faces. And they never forgot. Peter denied, but he came back. John went in "with Jesus" that terrible betrayal night. James was among the first to give up life for his Master. *We, too, need to see Jesus' glory.*

Monday.   Mark 9:11-18.
ARE WE FAILING SOMEBODY?
People expect much of Jesus' followers. They class us with him. What he did we can do, they think. They come to us expectantly, when we least think it. Without saying so, they bring their needs to us, their difficulties, temptations, hungry hearts, themselves. They expect something. They have a right to, too. *Are we failing* them? and Jesus? and ourselves? Then they quit expecting if they find we haven't anything. That's the worst failure of all.

19

Tuesday.   Mark 9:19-29.

THE UNFAILING JESUS.

But Jesus never failed anybody yet. The evil spirit tied like a whipped cur at his word. The demonized boy was released from his sore bondage. The broken-hearted father, relieved, overjoyed, hurried home with the boy to his mother. The critical, sneering crowd was forced to recognize the unmatched power of Jesus. It was *the close touch with his Father,* insisted upon, that turned the disciples' dismal failure into sweeping victory.

Wednesday.   Luke 9:30-37.

LET'S GO TO SCHOOL DAILY.

Prayer-touch with the Father—daily, openhearted, honest, unhurried, intimate, reverent touch—this is the secret of every needed thing. If we'd *go to school daily to God,* with the open Book, and learn how to pray, confidently, intelligently, like a child in simplicity, like a man in maturity, nothing could resist our touch. The life would be transfigured, and the service marked with God's own subtle, fragrant touch.

Thursday.   2 Kings 4:27-37.

LIVING A PRAYER.

When prayer takes hold of all there is of you, *you can take hold of all you will through prayer.* But prayer isn't saying religious words with your eyes shut and a terminal "amen" attached. Real prayer is a life. It begins as an act. It grows into a habit, then into a mental attitude. Then it becomes your very life. Then the man becomes the prayer. Such prayer can raise the dead, even now, into real life.

Friday.   Jas. 5:13-18.

WHEN THE MAN IS THE PRAYER.

Emergencies call for intense prayer. *When the man becomes the prayer* nothing can resist its touch. Elijah on Carmel, bowed down on the ground, with his face between his knees, that was the prayer—the man himself. No words are mentioned. Prayer can be too tense for words. The man's whole being was in touch with God, and was set with God against the powers of evil. They couldn't withstand such praying. There's more of this embodied praying needed.

Saturday.   2 Cor. 3:9-18.

SPIRIT PHOTOGRAPHY.

The eye is the soul of the face. The whole man looks out through the eye. You look into the man through his eye. *Give Jesus your eye with nothing between* you and him—no sin, no self-will, no prejudice, no self-seeking, no doubting, a full glad giving of the whole self daily in the fresh look up into his face—and he will come anew into you, and make you over into his own likeness.

Seventeenth Week

Sunday.   Mark 9:30-42.

A ROUGH SPELLING-LESSON.

Selfishness is the smoother way of spelling Satan. That sounds a bit rough; but it's true. The inner core of Satan is preferring himself to, yes, even to God; wanting everything for himself. Selfishness may be cultured and scholarly and polished (it's surprising how a coarse thing takes a high polish). Or, it may be coarse and brazen and open. But scratch it;

and you always find underneath the hooked Satan fingers reaching and holding.

Monday. Mark 9:43-50.

THE ONLY CURE FOR SELFISHNESS.
Selfishness is so ingrained in the human fiber that its cure takes fourfold treatment: a knife, a fluid, a fire, and salt. The knife of a strong purpose to cut it out; the blood of Jesus to wash it out; the fire of the Holy Spirit to burn it out; and *the salt of the Book brooded over,* and of the Spirit's indwelling, to spoil the soil so it has a hard time sprouting again.

Tuesday. Matt. 20:20-28.

LOVE IN THE FIRE.
Human love needs seasoning and tempering, refining and broadening, by the higher, deeper original love, the love of the heart of God. The stronger the human love, like a mother's, the truer this is. So it gets the clearer vision, the stronger purpose, the finer sacrificial traits of the God-love. And so whatever selfishness may have crept in, sometimes unconsciously. is burned out, and the love is sweeter yet when it gives instead of asking.

Wednesday. Luke 22:24-30.

UNCONSCIOUS GREATNESS.
True greatness never finds out that it is great. It is too much taken up thinking of others. When it finds out that it is great it ceases to be great. If you have discovered that you're humble, then you may know that you're not humble. For humility is so absorbed with the dear God, and with others, that it never knows it is humble. But *we'll never understand this till we've seen the face of Jesus.*

Thursday. 1 Cor. 13:1-13.

THE REAL HUMAN.
Love is a fire. It burns out the impurities, puts warmth in the heart and a gentle glow in the life. and tempers all to the best. God is love. *Man is love, too, when true to the image* in which he was made.

Jesus is love in human garb. To let Jesus in as a passion, the burning passion, is to have selfishness, with all its brood, burned out, and the true ideal made real. Then we live the life that blesses other lives.

Friday. Jas. 4:1-10.

A STUDY IN PROPORTIONS.
Humility is the foundation grace, the mother of all virtues and all strength. It does not mean thinking meanly of yourself and talking yourself down. It means *getting God in the right place.* Everything we have is from him. It is entrusted to us by him. It is at its best really only as it is used for him. When this gets hold of us it makes us friends of God, and crowds out every ungodlike thing.

Saturday. Isa. 28:1-7.

THERE'S SOMEONE HIDING BEHIND.
Strong drink is more than merely a drink. It's a doorway: one of Satan's; one of his favorite doorways for getting into a man's life. No, this isn't merely a strong way of putting the thing: this is really so. When the intoxicant, however mild, is taken in, the door is open for loose talk, loose morals, lost ideals, and all that brood. Letting the stuff severely alone is the only safe rule.

Sunday.   Mark 10:17-31.

LIFE AT FLOOD-TIDE.
A swift stream, at flood, frequently changes its channel, leaving the old, cutting out an entirely new bed. The Holy Spirit *floods the life with love* when he is allowed sway, Rom. 5:5, literal meaning. The old standards that can't stand the wash of this flood are left behind; new standards are set, flood-tide standards, with rich fertilizing silt, till we wonder how we ever lived the old way. And the upward tug of the new standards affects everything.

Monday.   Mark 10:1-12.

SHOES OFF, AND HAT, TOO.
Sin steals away reverence, and would make the finest things cheap and common. *Love hallows everything it touches*—real love. It reveals the sacredness of life's relationships. It puts a touch of tender awe, of thoughtful reverence, on the sacred intimacies, the holy privacies, of love and home and daily contacts, that hallows and enriches these, and holds them true to what should be. Reverence deepens as we see the working of God in nature's processes.

Tuesday.   Mark 10:13-16: Matt. 18:1-6.

SHAPING THE CHILD.
Children and women were commonly despised when Jesus came. He revealed their true worth and place. We need the children as really as they need us. Before the hurt of sin has come to them they teach us purity and simplicity, trust and honesty. They absorb their surroundings. *Children will be just what their elders are,* whom they touch daily. It's only as our lives are yielded wholly to Jesus' control that our children can come into their rightful heritage.

Wednesday.   Exod. 20:2-17.

THE GOD STANDARD.
Man needs a standard. The yardstick protects the seller from giving too much, and the buyer from getting too little. The ten practical Sinai Words give us the true standard of life on both positive and negative sides—what belongs in and what out. They begin with God and take in our neighbors and ourselves. *Putting God first makes the whole life ring true.* By his help we can keep him first, and so keep true.

Thursday.   Lev. 19:11-18.

GOD'S SIGNATURE.
God's signature of love and right is on every bit of true life. He is love. And love, as God lives it, is not a weak sentimentality of mere talk, but the most thoughtful, sane thing imaginable. It makes an exquisite blend of the practical and the ideal. It burns selfishness out. And getting selfishness out makes one thoughtful in a sane, practical way of everyone he touches, and about everything—and in his own daily life.

Friday.   Matt. 22:34-40.

STRAIGHTEN UP
Getting straight with God will make you straight with your next-door neighbor. The bother is that so much of our religion is of the pendulum kind; it swings this way and that, but, unlike a good clock, doesn't keep the balance true. God is love. Love is a flame. It reaches quietly, subtly, but effectively, up through the whole life; and outside, too. Nothing

within reach can escape its mellowing, shaping influence. It makes us good neighbors.

Saturday. Rom. 13:1-10.

THE LAW OF LOVE.

The law of love is the only satisfactory law. It fulfils every requirement of life because it fills up to the full all that should be, and it's a bubbling-over fulness, too, with the cup spilling out at the brim. Love is intelligent; it thinks. The brain is keener when the heart's afire with love. It thinks into what is due to others. It guards its own life. But there's more: it touches the will; it gives *power to reach the ideal.*

Nineteenth Week

Sunday. Mark 10:32-45.

LOVE AT CLIMAX.

Jesus felt the Cross. He felt it long before he reached it. Its shadow stretched far ahead and wrapped him in its black, clinging folds. He shrank from it. though he never flinched. The thorns tore, and the nails cut his heart, long before his body was touched by them. The shame of it stung to the quivering quick. Hut love held him steady. *If it only might grip us. how Jesus loved us!*

Monday. Mark 10:46-52.

PRACTICAL IDEALISM.

Jesus was a practical idealist. He had ideals, high ideals, the highest. He insisted upon them. Yet at every turn he was so simply, warmly practical. He was in the hurting-grip of his purpose to go to the Cross, yet he stopped at the cry of need. The whole world was filling his vision, yet the plea of a despised beggar stopped him. *Only the Jesus-touch makes practical idealists,* with broad vision and practical touch.

Tuesday. Zech. 13:1-9.

GOD'S MEMORY.

God never forgets. He couldn't. His love prevents it. Through the long wait of the centuries, and the terrible, unending tragedy of sin, he clings to his purpose. The cry of his heart over the world's need, and the ring of his insistent purpose to meet it, trail through the pages of the Book like the low sob of minor music out of a heart breaking with grief, yet holding steady in its inflexible purpose.

Wednesday. Isa. 53:1-12.

THE GOSPEL OF ISAIAH.

The 53d of Isaiah is the gospel in miniature. Jesus' human touch, his warm sympathy with us in our common experiences, the realness of his suffering both in life and in death, his patient steadiness in spite of cruel misunderstanding—especially of why he died, that it was for us, out of love—all this is told hundreds of years beforehand. And there's the gospel's glad sequel yet to come—its triumph through all the earth.

Thursday. Heb. 2:1-10.

FOR US.

The suffering of Jesus is distinctive in itself; quite apart from any other suffering. It was purely voluntary: the coming down here as he did, the lowly life he led, the suffering of spirit through his life, and the great climax—the Cross. It was all done of his own free accord for us. *He took our place and took what belonged to us.* This reveals the real love and meaning of Jesus' suffering.

Friday.   Phil. 2:1-11.

A GREAT MEETING.

The extremest extremes meet in Jesus. He came from the highest down to the lowest; then returned to the highest. The Son of God became the Son of man; the purest of men was treated as the worst; the freest as the bondservant of all; the most loving subjected to the bitterest hatred. But he gladly yielded, for so the worst can become purest, the slave free, and sons of men become sons of God.

Saturday.   Gal. 6:9-18.

THE FOCUS.

The whole of the gospel is in the Cross where Jesus died. The horribleness of sin, the hellishness of hate, the tenderness and tenacity of love, the superlative of sacrifice, the Father's passion for his world, the Son's unsparing devotion to the Father and to us, the one message for the world, the highest and truest passion of a human heart—all blend in that tremendous act when Jesus gave his life out to the death for us.

Twentieth Week

Sunday.   Mark 11:1-11.

CROWN HIM LORD OF ALL.

It was clear from the first that Jesus was a king. He had the royal lineage, the kingly power in helping people, kingly authority over evil, kingly graciousness with the people, wisdom in teaching, the innate sense of authority over his enemies. It was as a king that he hung upon the Cross, rose again out of death, and went back through the blue to his throne. And some day *lie is coming back* to reign over the earth.

Monday.   Mark 11:12-26.

ROYAL POWER.

Jesus is a king. And as we enthrone him habitually in our lives he exercises his kingly power: the bad is put out; a positive distaste for it is put in; and all the natural powers are breathed upon till they come to be at their best. The body is made strong, the mind keen and clear, the heart pure, the spirit strong; and love dominates all our contacts with others. Let's yield habitually to his kingly power.

Tuesday.   Mark 11:27-33.

KEEN YET GRACIOUS.

Jesus was never more alert mentally than when opposed. Enmity brought out some of the keenest things that he said. Yet he was never bitter, and never cut with mere sarcasm. There was ever *a wooing note of graciousness,* even when he denounced so terribly the hypocrisy of the Jerusalem leaders as he wept over the city. It's a great thing for us to note. His blended wisdom and love may be ours in the opposition we must meet.

Wednesday.   John 2:13-22.

STICK 'EM WITH IT!

When people doubt the sharpness of the edge of the Sword of the Spirit, don't argue, just stick 'em with it, gently but firmly; they'll find how sharp it is! When they question the power and love of Jesus, get them in contact with him. That'll fix their questions. He revealed his power to these critical Jews by his actions. And he will today as we let him speak and act through our lips and lives.

Thursday. Ps. 45:1-11.
KINGLY KINDNESS.
Graciousness is the characteristic kingly trait. Yet true graciousness never compromises on the right. Jesus was "full of grace *and* truth." Not grace without truth; that is a weak sentimentality. Not truth without grace; that is hard and repellant. Truth is grace holding up the highest standard and insisting on its being reached. Grace is truth reaching down a strong arm and helping you attain the standard. Jesus was full of both. This is his kingliness.

Friday. Zech. 9:9-17.
THE COMING BIRTHDAY.
God has a wondrous ideal for the old earth. He has never forgotten it amid all the tangle and confusion and strife down here. There's a glad day coming. It will be *a new birthday for the earth,* the day of birth into a new life. It comes with the coming of the King. Jesus' coming is not the end of the world, but the beginning of the better order. Lord Jesus, come quickly. The world needs to recognize and obey its King.

Saturday. 1 Cor. 3:16-23.
OPENING THE DOOR.
What does it mean to be a Christian? To believe the Bible? No. It's far simpler and more radical. It means this: *opening the door of your life to Jesus,* and letting him have full sway. When that's done he comes in, and reshapes the whole life on the shape of his own presence. Then you believe the Bible from lid to lid because you have Jesus. When you have him you believe it and you love it.

Twenty-First Week

Sunday. Mark 12:1-12.
SELFISHNESS IS SUICIDAL.
The Jews rejected Jesus, the Son of God and their own and the world's rightful King. And so they rejected their opportunity to be the world's first nation. "They left him"; utterly, severely, they *left* him. And so he was forced to leave them. That's always the order. If ever God leaves a man it is only long after the man has left God. Sin is suicidal. *Selfishness nails its own coffin.* Rejection of Jesus is self-rejection.

Monday. Mark 12:13-17, 28-34.
THE BAD IS WEAKER.
Satan is no match for God. Bad can't hold its own against good in an even contest. *No opposition can stand up against Jesus.* It is only God's patience with men that makes evil seem so powerful in the present contest. God is determined that men shall have fullest opportunity. His patience is beyond words. Ours should be Jesus, in control in our lives, will hold his own and more against all ridicule and opposition that we meet.

Tuesday.   Mark 12:35-44.

THE JESUS POISE.

The heart should join with the mind in holding the reins of the life. They ought to drive abreast, not tandem. Then lips and purse and life will ring true, and ring together. Not the heart without the head; not the head without the heart; each balancing the other: all the powers working in unison. This reveals the Jesus touch, and gives the Jesus poise. But it's possible really, practically, only as Jesus is in control.

Wednesday.   Ps. 2:1-12.

THE DAY.

Some day man's opportunity will have had full run. God's patience will have endured the tangle of earth to the full for man's sake. Then the King will rise up from his seat. He will step into action anew on the earth. lie will put an end to the control of evil, clean up the earth, right the wrong, and heal the broken-hearted. *We hasten the glad day* by being true now to the King.

Thursday.   Ps. 116:1-14.

LOVE BREEDS LOVE.

Our love to God grows out of his love for us. He does so much for us. We may forget him, but he never forgets any man. He gives us our breath continuously; else our lives would quickly snuff out. He gives us bed and bread, shelter of roof, warmth of fire, sunshine and rain. He gave his Son's blood for us on Calvary. *If a man stop to think* even a bit, the answering love must come.

Friday.   1 Pet. 2:13-25.

HUMAN GOVERNMENTS.

All government represents God, whether of city or state or nation. It may not be wise always, nor just, nor fair. We should do our full share as citizens, when the opportunity comes, to make it the best possible. But without it, even at its worst, life would be unlivable. It stands for God's authority, however inadequately. And we should, as his true followers, give full obedience to the Government, except when an instructed conscience forbids.

Saturday.   2 Cor. 8:9-15.

THE DEBT OF LOVE.

The Jew was taxed a tenth, and made freewill offerings besides. All the Christian has belongs to God. Whatever we have is his, because *we* are his. It is given us in trust, to be administered conscientiously as his Spirit suggests. We are to owe no man anything. Yet *we are badly in debt.* It is a debt of love, due to God, payable to man. We pay it only by giving freely as the Spirit directs.

Twenty-Second Week

Sunday.   Mark 13:1-9.

THE SADDEST THING.

The saddest thing is to be untrue to God's plan for one's life. The Jewish Temple was the heart of the Jewish nation. It enshrined all that the nation stood for. It represented the national ideal—faithfulness to God and to their God-given world-mission. They were untrue to God and to their world-mission. So they were destroyed as a nation (not as a people). But they are to have another chance. The patience of God!

Monday. Mark 14:1-9.

LOVE-HUNGRY.

Jesus is so grateful for love. It alone can satisfy his heart. He judges everyone by the heart's action. He thinks of every action of ours, every bit of service, every gift, by how much heart is in it. It's the coin, or the act, that is tinged red with the heart's blood, which he prizes most. It may be only a small jar of ointment, but its fragrance fills his heart and all the world.

Tuesday. Mark 13:31-37.

THE STIMULUS OF LOVE.

Love is keen. No eyes so sharply alert as love's eyes; no brain so wide-awake as the brain stimulated by love. It's only when the heart's aflame with a tender love that the mind and ear and eye and hand are at their best. When it's a dear friend you're watching for, then all the life is on tiptoe. It isn't simply watching; it's watching for *him!* And the watching makes sooner the day of the coming.

Wednesday. Ezek. 33:1-11.

SALTY SALT.

The world needs Christians even when it refuses their Christ. Salt is the great pre-servative. We are the world's salt. Our presence has a wholesome influence. It is of utmost importance *to keep this salt really salty.* Watchfulness. in a sane, wholesome way, to be ready when our Lord may return—this tends to keep the whole life true. And this not only bears witness to the world; it also helps the world, even when the witness is rejected.

Thursday. John 11:47-57.

"WATCH—"

The world spirit hasn't changed since Jesus was here. It conspired against him with devilish cunning and persistence, and it conspires against his followers today. The mode of attack may change, but not the impelling motive behind it. You can suffocate the life out of a man in a hogshead of molasses. We need to be on our guard against that evil world spirit, with gracious tactfulness in all personal contacts, but keenly alert against the attack.

Friday. Matt. 9:9-13.

HAVE YOU FOUND IT OUT?

We are all sinners, but most of us haven't found it out; at least, not to the point of feeling what a desperate fix we're in, and how much it cost Jesus, of blood and pain, to be our friend. And so we don't really come to Jesus; our Christianity is of the formal sort. When we do find it out we're eager to come, and to come all the way. And *Jesus gladly receives all who come.*

Saturday. John 14:21-28.

CAN YOU SPELL?

Can you spell? Do you know the other way of spelling love? Put the "o" first, then a "b," an "e," and a "y," and you get the practical day-by-day meaning. Yet "obey" doesn't mean merely doing things. Obedience is *the rhythm of our wills with Jesus' will.* It opens the way for him to pour out the fulness of his love, and this in turn stirs ours to a new depth and tenderness. Let us learn the spelling that links our lives to his.

Sunday. Mark 14:17-26.

KEPT EVER FRESH.

On the very eve of Judas' faithlessness, and of his own suffering, Jesus was thinking of others. He was planning that by the taking of sacred bread and the cup, in the coming years, in the midst of persecution and temptation, of hardship and ease, we might ever keep fresh in mind his deathless, dying love. Even so, *if the heart's attuned,* every breaking of common bread may remind us of him, and help to hold us true.

Monday. Luke 22:3-6. 21-23, 47-49.

JUDAS ISN'T SO LONELY.

Judas stands out through history as a man utterly despised because he betrayed his friend, and, worse yet, who did it by the use of friendship's token of love. But—but—be careful, there, in talking about Judas! Is he so lonely after all? He simply put self-interest first, even though it meant putting Jesus second; no, not second—clear out! Is this so uncommon? Judas did not realize how much it meant. Does anyone realize what *his* faithlessness may mean?

Tuesday. John 13:21-30.

THE INSIDE KNOB.

It is startling to think that Satan can actually come into the heart of a man in such close touch with Jesus as Judas was. And more—he is cunningly trying to do it today. Yet he can get in only through a door opened from the inside. *Every man controls the door of his own life.* Satan can't get in without our help. Master, help me keep my door tightly shut against him, and all his crafty wiles.

Wednesday. Mark 14:27-42.

INTENSEST ANTICIPATION.

The spirit battle of Calvary was fought out in Gethsemane. There the realization came in upon Jesus, with the greatest intensity yet, that on the morrow he was to be *treated as sin should be.* The nightmare horror of it to his sinless soul well-nigh snapped the life-cord. But he never flinched. He yielded to the Father's plan for our salvation, even though it meant such suffering. Blessed Jesus!

Thursday. Mark 14:43-45,66-72.

WITH JESUS?

It was the inner circle that failed Jesus in the crisis—those who knew him best and companioned with him most. This is terrible. Peter denied; Judas betrayed; nine ran away; but John went in "with Jesus" into the thickest of the danger, at the possible risk of his own life. We must always be grateful for clear John. There was one who didn't fail. But the crisis isn't over yet. *Are any of us failing Jesus?*

Friday. 2 Cor. 11:21-33.

HE'LL LIFT THE LATCH FOR US.

Paul followed where the Spirit led. This was his unchanging rule. Satan did his best and worst to block the road, and turn Paul back. And he is still working in the same way, with accumulated experience. The roadway of obedience he still makes hard; sometimes seemingly impossible. But *there's a gate at the end of every blind alley.* And the Holy Spirit will lift the latch for us as we follow close regardless of obstacles and hardships.

Saturday.   Matt. 10:24-33.

NOT SO ROUGH.

When the road's rough, sharp stones cutting your feet, steep up-hill pull, brow a bit moist, jaw shut, hand clenched, it helps us to remember this: Jesus was here; he trod this same way. He was here *first,* and he was here *most.* It's never so rough since his feet have smoothed it down. And he is in it today, close by the one who holds steady in spite of the roughness. Let's lean on Jesus a bit harder.

Twenty-Fourth Week

Sunday.   Mark 15:1-11.

CAMOUFLAGE. BE WARY!

The issue is always sharply drawn between evil and good, Barabbas and Jesus. On the face of it, it would seem that there is no issue. Most of us would promptly reject Satan and accept Jesus. But the cunningness of it today is that *evil wears a beautiful false-face.* There needs to be not only the decision to choose Jesus and always ring true to him, but also the open eye and the trained ear, that we may recognize Satan's disguises.

Monday.   Mark 15:12-20.

NO LITTLE THINGS.

You can never tell how much your "yes" or "no" may mean. Pilate didn't realize the tremendous significance of his consent to the crucifying of Jesus. To him perhaps it was simply one case more, unusually troublesome, to be gotten rid of. But *there are no little things* when right and wrong are at stake. The tendency today is to slip along the easiest way, as Pilate did. Jesus, Master, help us to ring true to thee in all things.

Tuesday.   Mark 15:22-39.

TWO STORIES IN ONE.

The Cross spells out two stories: one in black, ugly pot-black, the story of sin. Sin carpentered the cross, and wove the thorns, and drove the nails: *our sin.* And a story, too, in red, bright-flowing red, the story of love, *his love,* that yielded to cross and nails and shame for us. And only the passion of his love burning within will make us hate sin, as only his blood can wash it out.

Wednesday.   Matt. 27:39-56.

THE HIGHEST PEAK.

The hill of the Cross is the highest hill on earth in its significance. There hate's worst and love's best met, and *love won.* Jesus was victorious as he yielded to the pain and shame of the Cross. He did it freely of his own accord. He did it out of love. He did it for us. So, and only so, are we safe and saved. May the love of it grip us anew today!

Thursday.   Matt. 27:57-66.

THE LOWEST VALLEY.

Jesus' burial was the climax of his death, as the death was the climax of his life. Joseph's tomb, carefully sealed with imperial Rome's mark, tied the knot on the end of the thread of his death. There could now be no doubt that he had really died. His death touched the very bottom. He went to the very lowest, *putting death to death for us,* and making the new life as real as the death was. Because of the

Friday. Isa. 53:1-13.

THE ROUGHEST ROAD.

It was a long road that Jesus came down to us in our sin, and a rough road, too. There were the crossed logs right across the road, and they were all overgrown with the sharp thorns and the poison ivy. But this couldn't hold Jesus back. for *he was thinking of us.* And he pushed his way through, bearing the scars to this very hour. But he reached the world, and he has reached our hearts. It was hard for him, but how good for us!

Saturday. Rom. 5:1-11.

ON THE JESUS LEVEL.

Now, we're reckoned *as pure and right as Jesus is.* On the cross he was reckoned as bad and stubborn and unclean as we are in our sin. Now, blessed be his wondrous Name, we are reckoned as he is. We are taken into the Father's home and heart as Jesus himself was: accepted in the Beloved. Because he went down to the lowest, we can be taken up to the highest.

Twenty-Fifth Week

Sunday. Mark 16:1-11.

THE CENTER OF SPIRIT GRAVITY.

Death is a result of sin. There was no sin in Jesus. Death had no power over him. Fur a great love-purpose he yielded to it. Then, when the great errand was done, he yielded to the natural upward gravity of his sinless life, and rose up, up through the rock of the tomb, up into life, a new life, a new sort of life. So it will be with us when he comes back.

Monday. Mark 16:12-20.

THE OLIVET OUTLOOK.

We should pitch our tents on Olivet's top. That grove of trees yonder, that's Gethsemane; a bit farther beyond, that's Calvary; up north there lies white Hermon, where the inner glory looked out. This is the Olivet landscape. But here is Jesus himself standing, face looking *out;* hand pointing *out;* words ringing *out: "Go ye"*—all of you go, go to all. This is the ringing cry, until Jesus' feet again press Olivet's top.

Tuesday. John 21:15-25.

FINDING OUR FEET.

Peter had lost his footing. Jesus had died; that had stunned him. He had risen; that had stupefied him with joy. But he didn't know what to do. Then, after failing at his old job, there's a sight of Jesus, there's obedience to his command, and the talk about love. These are the things we need: a vision of Jesus, empowered, *in our midst;* a spirit of obedience to him; a heart of tender love in all our personal contacts.

Wednesday. 1 Cor. 15:1-11.

THE UNSEEN COMRADE.

The disciples had no doubt about Jesus having risen. They were walking along the country road, sitting at the supper table, gathered in the sitting-room of that Jerusalem home, in the boat on Galilee's blue waters: each time they were talking about him but hadn't any thought of his being there. Then, each time, they found him in their midst. Even so *he is with us* as we are talking and thinking of him. Let's recognize his presence.

Thursday. 1 Cor. 15:50-58.
THE LAST ENEMY.
It's natural to shrink from death. Death's an enemy. It's unnatural. But when Jesus is allowed sway in our hearts, there's victory over the enemy. He fills us so full of himself and keeps us so busy telling others of him, that the fear is clean crowded out. *We shall sing, because of Jesus, even when death comes closest.* Then some day the full victory will come, and death itself will be put to death.

Friday. 1 Thess. 4:13-18.
THE DOORWAY IN THE BLUE.
Some day there'll be *a break in tine blue overhead.* It'll be followed by *a break in the brown underfoot.* As Jesus comes back again through that doorway of the blue, our believing loved ones who have been laid away under the sod will rise again, and we who are living and trusting Jesus will join them and be caught up into the presence of the glorified Jesus. It may be sooner than we think. Lord Jesus, come quickly.

Saturday. Rev. 21:1-8.
GOD'S GARDEN.
God never forgets. He never fails. His gift of free choice made sin possible. Sin broke up Eden, and has made sad havoc. But Jesus has died for sin. Patiently God is waiting that every man may have fullest opportunity. But he hasn't forgotten. He holds his ideal close to his great heart, and some day it will be made real. We shall all live in God's garden with the Father—except those who refuse to come in.

Twenty-Sixth Week

Sunday. Psalm 2.
OUR KINGLY KINSMAN.
The quarter's title tells the whole story: *Jesus,* that's the man, our brother, who shared our experiences, and can sympathize; *Christ,* that's the "anointed one," the chosen of the Father to make real his great ideal for man; *Redeemer,* that's our kinsman who gave his blood to buy us back out of sin's slavery; *Lord,* that's the one who comes in to hold sweet mastery in our personal lives. And *our,* that ties him and us hard together.

Monday. Matt. 15:29-38.
OUR PART IN THE PARTNERSHIP.
Jesus sets us actually free by his own transfiguring presence. With his blood he purges out the sin that enslaves. By his Spirit he kindles his own fires on the hearthstone of our hearts, and the flames burn up the bonds of selfishness and prejudice. His own presence mellows and then molds, constantly, patiently, quietly, until we are transfigured from the hurt of sin back to his own image. Our part is the full, thoughtful, habitual yielding to him.

Tuesday. Matt. 18:1-10.
THE RAREST OF THINGS.
Poise is The rarest of things in actual life—poise of opinion, poise of character, poise of religious conviction. It avoids extremes at both ends. Jesus had the rarest poise. And the man actually swayed by the Jesus spirit will grow gradually into the same poise. The negative and positive traits will balance as they should. Selfishness, prejudice, self-will will be put out. Love as a practical passion will set the standard in all things.

Wednesday.   Luke 18:24-34.

THE GREAT MASTER.

Jesus was King even in his dying. He was masterly, not only in his life, but as he approached the cross and then hung upon it. A strong purpose held him calm, steady, victorious, as he walked deliberately toward the greatest suffering of spirit and body ever borne, and accomplished the tremendous thing he had set himself to do. This tells how some clay he'll rule the world, and meanwhile our lives as we yield to him.

Thursday.   Luke 20:39-47.

LEARNING SPEECH AND SILENCE.

Jesus' enemies couldn't answer his words nor withstand his power. With speech, masterly in its simplicity and keenness and rare insight into their motives, and with power, silent, intangible, but utterly resistless, he held off their hands of hate reaching for Jerusalem stones as at the Nazareth precipice, until his chosen hour had come for yielding. And if he may have habitual sway in us, *he will teach our lips both speech and silence,* and shield our persons.

Friday.   Mark 14:46-50, 60-62.

DON'T BE AFRAID.

Jesus was fearless. He knew ahead about Judas' dastardly betrayal, Peter's cowardly denial, and the frightened flight of the rest—the collapse of those nearest. He saw with painful distinctness the shadows of the cross growing blacker on his path. He felt it all keenly, as none other ever felt such experiences. Yet he calmly faced them. He was never afraid. Perfect confidence in the Father and passionate love for men *kept fear clean out:* and will for us.

Saturday.   Matt. 28:1-10.

NO DEFEAT WITHOUT CONSENT.

Jesus was triumphant *in* all his experiences, as well as *over* them: in the commonplace, tiresome carpenter-shop round; the wilderness temptation, so tense and subtle; the ceaseless nagging persecutions; under the deeply shadowed olive trees; before shifty, powerful Pilate; and on the dread cross, as well as when his triumph is so apparent in the Resurrection and Ascension. And so may we be. By Jesus' grace *no one can be defeated without his own consent.*

Twenty-Seventh Week

Sunday.   Acts 16:13-24.

THE HELPFULNESS OF SNAGS.

Do we sometimes forget that our Lord said that persecutions would come? The evil one resents being interfered with. He puts snags in our way. We may have to suffer for the right. But persecutions, even though they be hard to bear, need never discourage. They tell that our way doesn't suit Satan. When they come let's hold steady; when the snags are thickest it is time for the promises to be realized.

Monday.   Acts 16:25-34.

SINGING IN A BLIND ALLEY.

When the heart believes, it sings, no matter what contrary signs or circumstances there are. The expectant heart prays *and* sings. We all pray when we are in a tight place; but do we sing, too? If you really expected the walls of your tight corner to break, wouldn't you be singing all the day? And when the walls break, look out for those whom you face—they may be needing you to point them to Him who saves.

Tuesday. John 1:35-42.

SIGNPOSTS NEEDED.
John was like a signpost pointing to Jesus. A signpost may seem insignificant—just a common bit of wood stuck up. But it's a great thing; for it shows the right way. We don't question signposts; we go the way they point. Let's have the sign of Christ so clear upon our lives that men will go straight to him, with never a doubt as to which is the right way.

Wednesday. John 1:43-51.

HOW TO FIND THE TRUTH ABOUT JESUS.
Nathanael heard about Jesus. He might have just stayed where he was, and "listened on." How many of us just "listen on"! But merely listening about Jesus keeps him waiting. When we start toward him, he sees us coming, and speaks to us just where he finds us. And he never fails to satisfy the heart. Then we know it is really he; for no mere man ever really meets and satisfies us just where we know we are.

Thursday. Acts 2:37-47.

CUT OUT THE "IF."
When we learn about Jesus, we realize it was our sin that hurt him to the death. And the natural question is, "What shall we do about it?" When we let him have his way, he makes us share instead of hoarding. So we give him a channel. And he is a God who doeth wonders when he has a channel. He (lid wonders through these Apostles. He will eagerly do wonders all the time, everywhere, if—.

Friday. Matt. 25:14-30.

THE LIFE IN BETWEEN.
What did the man with the one talent do after he had buried it? He had a talent. He buried it. Then there came the end. But the life in between? Was it spent in selfish interest and gain? Let's be careful to keep ever in sight the thing our Master asks us to do. If we let things come in to cover up our vision of him and his plan—that'll be a bad burial.

Saturday. John 15:8-16.

A PLANNED LIFE.
It is a high ideal that Jesus sets for the life. And he takes us into close, confidential friendship about it all. He tells us what he expects, and how it may be. When we are his friends, and he tells what that means, he makes clear his plan that our life and prayers are to count in the changing of things that need changing, and in the bringing to pass of things that ought to happen.

Twenty-Eighth Week

Sunday. Acts 8:26-39.

LIVING THE BOOK OPENS IT.
Written words always have the power of their source. That is why Cod's Word is so wonderful. Even when you do not quite understand it you feel its power. It is a blessed thing to have the personal touch with the Man of the Book. Only so can one understand it,

and help others to. And we never do understand his Word until we begin to live it. Living it opens it.

Monday. Ps. 19:7-14.

EAT THE BOOK.

David says wonderful things about God's Word. We believe it. But believing isn't enough. We all believe that food builds up the body. But if we stopped there, we'd be weak and emaciated. Food must both be taken in and lived out in action. Then it does its work in the body. If we take in the Word and live it out, it will refresh us, throw light on the path, give wisdom and strength, and lead to victory.

Tuesday. Ps. 119:9-16.

THE PROOF OF THE BOOK.

We do forget, unless we have the same reasons for remembering that the psalmist speaks of before his last sentence. Let's read this portion over again with that in mind. He must have found out the truth of God's Word by living it, for he says he will delight himself in God's rules for his life. We don't forget the things we take delight in. The proof of the Book is the delight of it.

Wednesday. Ps. 119:97-105.

TASTE AND SEE.

God's Word tells the power there is in it for whoever will. And whoever *will* let it change the life, and meet the need of the life, will love it. A thing is dear to us in proportion to our appreciation of its worth. He who knows the power of God's Word in the personal life when the way is difficult, loves it. We don't *know* whether a thing is sweet till we taste it, nor whether it is lovable till we test it.

Thursday. . Matt. 7:24-27.

DISBELIEF DOESN'T ALTER FACTS.

Truth is not affected by whether one believes it or not. God tells us in his Word what is right. He tells us the consequences of obedience and also of disobedience. The decision always lies in one's own power of choice. Most of us hear; fewer of us seem to do the thing we know. Why is it? Is it because the evil one opposes anyone who hears God's Word? Let's strive *to do all we know*

Friday. Luke 24:25-32.

OBEDIENCE AFFECTS THE EYE.

Jesus is faithful. He still opens his Word to the eager listener. As of old the heart burns, for his brooding presence in the Book gives light and clears the meaning. To the willing mind and heart the Book opens clearly and distinctly. It is only to him who is willing to do that the life-plan is made plain.

> "Light obeyed increaseth light,
> Light rejected bringeth night."

Obedience is the open door to the Book.

Saturday. 2 Tim. 3:10-17.

THE SHEET ANCHOR.

We need not be depressed. No matter what happens we can absolutely reckon on Jesus and his Word. It means so much that he has told us how things will go, else we should be wondering, maybe absorbed with wondering, about the evil things all around about, and the trials of our own life. As we obey him and lean unquestioningly upon his pledged Word, we shall know afresh the wondrous power of the Book.

Twenty-Ninth Week

Sunday.   Luke 11:1-13.

THINGS HAPPEN.

When we know Jesus we are perfectly confident that he hears us. He is so eager to have us come, with our hearts pure and our prayers insistent against the opposition of the evil one. And Jesus has never yet failed anyone who has asked out of an obedient life and an insistence against the power of the evil one. When we forgive even as we desire forgiveness, and expect because of Jesus' blood, things happen.

Monday.   Ps. 145:8-19.

OUR OBEDIENCE HELPS GOD.

It is a sweet thing to read about how close God is. But when you know him personally, and are conscious of his presence, so that he is the most real of all realities, then the heart understands this psalm of praise. It is the obedient life that knows. Obeying him opens his hand; obedience to him results in our desires being fulfilled. Obey, and you'll never be disappointed in him, and you'll be singing psalms, and talking of his power.

Tuesday.   Matt. 7:7-14.

THE PRAYER HINGE.

We read about "ask," "seek," "knock," and the definite results. It sounds beautiful, easy, thus far. But there are always conditions. We all want results. And he wants us to have the results. That is why he tells us so plainly how to live so that our prayers will *get* and *find* and *open*. The prayer hinges on the life. The life hinges on obedience. Obedience hinges on a set purpose *and* his grace.

Wednesday.   Acts 12:1-12.

THE UNSEEN IS MIGHTIER.

Faith does not reckon on things seen but on things unseen. Prison and chains and armed guards would be circumstances that would seem unalterable. Who does not know a hard-pressed situation when everything seems bound tight against us? But there need be no prison nor chain nor guard on one's spirit. One may always pray. Peter's body became as free as was his spirit, and he walked out from prison and chain and guard. So may we—if we will.

Thursday.   Isa. 55:1-9.

TAKE GOD AT HIS WORD.

We don't quite understand about the marvelous words of life. The mind seems stupid about spiritual things. But when we take God at his word, then such realities take place that the mind's stupidity clears as a fog lifts before the sun's shining. His ways are higher than our ways, but when we take him at his word, we are lifted up to the level of his ways. Then we know whom we have believed.

Friday.   Phil. 4:4-9.

THE SONG IN YOUR HEART.

The spirit of prayer is the close touch with himself that brings us into the place of God's own peace. It is a peace passing our understanding, but not our possession. With such peace could you be anxious? or fail to talk over everything with him? Some of us miss that peace because we do not learn the truth and do it. Jesus shows us the truth, and how to live it.

Saturday.   Ps. 46:1-11.
BE STILL AND FIND GOD.
That word "present" in this psalm is so close and warm. Even though mountains and waters are disturbed, and though the very earth itself shakes up, *we'll be still* and *know* that he is God, because he says so, and because we find it's true. In the stress of things just now let's remember that he is our help, close and strong. We cannot realize the strength of his presence until we grow quiet in the midst of earth's noises and storms.

Thirtieth Week

Sunday.   Matt. 4:17-22.
FAILING GOD HINDERS HIS PLAN.
Flow glad we are that Peter and Andrew obeyed Jesus when he spoke to them! There is somebody, yes, many, who will be grateful if *we* will but obey when Jesus speaks to us. Every failure to obey hurts God's plan. It hurts his plan for us and through us. Sometimes he says, "Stay with the nets." If so, he faithful. Sometimes he says, "Leave the nets," and if so, let's do it.

Monday.   John 14:15-24.
YOU .CAN *WILL* TO LOVE.
We have neither the disposition nor the power to obey our Lord until we love him first and most of all. His presence within gives power to overcome the opposition to his will. And love makes the heart more fit for his indwelling. When we know Jesus we love him. And love always delights in pleasing the one loved. If we have any trouble obeying, let's get better acquainted with Jesus. He is always wooing us with loving-kindness.

Tuesday.   Jas. 1:19-27.
DO IT!
We know only what we experience. We cannot know the truth of God's Word until we do it. The reason why some doubt the power of Jesus, both for personal victory and for helping others, is because they have stopped short of doing. Thinking religious thoughts and approving them is not enough. "Whatsoever he saith unto you, do it." Only so can there be victory in the life, and power through the life with those whom we touch.

Wednesday.   John 15:8-17.
LOVE WHEN YOU CAN'T LIKE.
We may not be able always to agree, but if we keep the heart full of warm, tender love for others, we shall be able to see matters from another's angle as well as our own. Lack of love shuts out sympathy, and shortens the vision, and loses the poise. And let's remember that we can love even when we find it impossible to like. The soul of any man is lovable, though his ways may not be.

Thursday.   Ps. 103:13-22.
KEEP THE NEEDLE STEADY.
God's Word is full of beautiful promises, and they lead us to fascinating results. Results

are magnetic. The needle-point of our desire turns their way. But there are always *conditions*. Conditions unfulfilled keep the needle-point on the wabble; fulfilled, hold it true to its object. Remembering his precepts to *do* them steadies the needle-point: it points true and straight to the results that are surely coming. When we are absorbed with obedience the results are bound to come.

Friday.   Mic. 6:1-8.

NOT THINGS. BUT—.

It is not things that our God wants. He wants *us*. And when we yield ourselves in glad obedience to him, his Spirit lives in us and reaches through us; it is *himself* in us, acting through our wills, who accomplishes what God requires. When he has his way in the life, it means, first, a possession; then, a reshaping. And that makes our mental processes wise and just and kindly, and so all the *acts* of life.

Saturday.   1 John 2:1-6.

THE LIFE LIVED OUT.

It cost Jesus his life poured out to walk among us and to redeem us from the guilt and power of sin. It will cost us our life *lived out* in obedience to his every word, to walk as he walked and have victory over sin. For walking as he walked is obeying. He showed us the way by going in it. Then he asks us to follow him, and tells us what will be the blessed consequences.

Thirty-First Week

Sunday.   Luke 2:42-52.

THE LIFE MUST FOLLOW THE VISION.

There is no standing still in life. Jesus came in touch with the teachers, and his heart and life opened in response. He awakened, and he matured. Many times one is awakened, but instead of maturing, the life just halts, and a halt of that kind means a dulling vision. The life must follow close to the vision, else we lose instead of gaining in strength.

Monday.   2 Pet. 1:1-8.

HOW'S YOUR TAPROOT?

Faith is the taproot of the Christian life. It goes deep into Jesus, out from whom come all the promises for growth and fruitage. The fruit tree roots deep down. When leaves and blossoms appear in the spring, we know the root is active; then we may indeed expect fruit. When the life shows forth patience, loving-kindness, self-control, and a Christ-likeness, then we know it roots down deep in Jesus. If not—well, there's a big question, to say the least.

Tuesday.   Eph. 6:10-20.

HOW TO FIGHT.

There is an enemy. And he opposes anyone who enters the "follow-me" road. It's immensely helpful to know just who it is that opposes. Not a man merely, nor the circumstances we see and feel. We may be gentle with the man, and patient under the circumstances, while we fight against the evil spirit foe concealed in or back of them. And this is our fighting—pleading Jesus' blood, and pleading persistently until victory comes.

Wednesday.   Col. 1:3-11.

REAL PREACHING.

When the truth of God gets into the heart, things change. We become bigger in size, better in quality, and purer in heart. Truth is an active principle. And that change inside *gets out to others.* We grow stronger in life, more sympathetic with others, more helpful in personal contact. And the big, luscious fruit hanging over the wall attracts the crowd on the street of life to the "Husbandman" that can make such fruit grow.

Thursday.   Isa. 40:25-31.

STRENGTH ENOUGH TO WAIT.

When we learn to wait for our Lord's lead in everything, we shall know the strength that finds *its climax in an even, steady walk.* Many of us are lacking in the strength we so covet. But God gives full power for every task he appoints. Waiting, holding oneself true to his lead—this is the secret of strength. And anything that falls out of the line of obedience is a waste of time and strength. Watch for his leading.

Friday.   Eph. 3:14-21.

THE PIVOT'S INSIDE.

It's blessed to know that he is *able* to do so much more than we ask or think, and that he *will.* His love is even more than his power. Our asking and. thinking seem so big sometimes; we stagger a bit with the thought of his doing quite that much. But listen: it is according to the power working *in* us. When he is allowed to work as he will on the inside, there'll be no bother about the outside.

Saturday.   Phil. 4:10-16.

PROVE IT; THEN TEACH IT.

Paul is talking out of experience in these words. That's why they mean so much. It is useless to talk about Christ's power, unless back of the words there is the actual experience that knows that that power is real, dependable. Paul believed Jesus; he squared his life to Jesus' teaching. That is why he could do all things in Jesus' strength. Jesus' strength was in Paul. Paul did things, but the power was from Jesus.

Thirty-Second Week

Sunday.   Luke 10:25-37.

LIVING IT FIRST.

We'll always find that whatever Jesus asks us to do, he has done. He has done it first, and he has done it most. He has shown us the way to do it. When we help others let us do it his way, and for his sake. The motive in one's action determines the power in it. If our helping others is for his sake, there's an added touch of help over and above the thing done.

Monday.   Gal. 6:1-10.

DO YOU UNDERSTAND?

Love understands. When Jesus' love controls the life, it makes the heart full of the sympathy that thinks and understands. A heart like his is quick arid gentle with the one needing help, because it understands. It reaches in to the human spirit. It eases the strain and stress of the heavy load, because it understands how to unload hurts and griefs and cares. We all love the human touch and sympathy. *True sympathy is ability to understand.*

Tuesday. Matt. 22:34-40.
NO GAPS. PLEASE.
We are to give God the devotion of our whole life. Our life is to be lived straight out and on in following unswervingly after him. We are not to start his way and then take a day off in the direction of self-interest. If we do, perplexities and doubts thicken with every step. The secret of the true life is bound up in the unfaltering purpose to please him perfectly. And *love of him begets love for others.*

Wednesday. 1 Cor. 13:1-13.
A SPELLING LESSON.
We marvel at the life Jesus lived and gave for us. One word explains it all: his love. What is love? Trace Jesus' steps; then you will know. The practical spelling of love is J-e-s-u-s. *We know it only as we know him.* It was his love that gave meaning to everything said and done. No matter what talents we have, the real thing's lacking unless love's the driving power within. The rest makes statistics chiefly.

Thursday. 1 John 3:13-22.
DO YOU DO IT?
When Jesus died for us, it wasn't because we were lovable. It was because we were so deeply tangled in sin. And our sin had to be got rid of somehow, it was hurting us so. It is easy to love the lovable. He loved us when we were unlovable. When we love the unlovable, even if we cannot like them, and are even willing to give our lives daily to win them, that's the real touch of the real Jesus spirit.

Friday. Rom. 12:1-9.
—FOUND YOUR PLACE IN THE PLAN?
We are to be content with what we are appointed to do, and do it singingly, with singleness of purpose. Any bit of service Jesus appoints is a privilege. It is a temptation to get fascinated with somebody else's privilege or gift, and long to be able to do likewise. That steals away the joy, and keeps us from finding *our place in his plan.* And to miss our place in his plan is to be like a derelict steamer adrift in mid-ocean.

Saturday. Rom. 12:10-21.
GET THE RESULT.
True service is so intent upon the result that the personal honor of having a part is quite forgot. If another can do the part better, we'll prefer the other, and we'll pray for him as he does it better. It's the result that we're after. And when we are yoked up in service, we are to be as Jesus was when he served with others. He came not to criticize but to help, to get the result needed.

Thirty-Third Week

Sunday. Acts 2:41-47.
THE REAL CHURCH.
The Church is really composed of all those who have opened their hearts to Jesus. They are joined together by the Holy Spirit dwelling in them. They are chiefly concerned about one thing—getting men everywhere to know that Jesus came down and lived and loved and died. So living together and working together there comes a renewal of strength, and there goes a clear, ringing witness to the world of the power of Jesus.

Monday. Acts 4:32-37.

THE JESUS INSTINCT.

When we get a vision of Jesus we know that all we have is *from* him. We know it belongs *to* him. It is ours only in trust, to be used *for* him. And we are willing and eager so to use it that his message of love may be loosed out to draw others to him. The common instinct is to keep all for ourselves. The Jesus instinct is to use it so men shall know about him.

Tuesday. Acts 6:1-7.

NOT HOW MUCH BUT HOW WELL.

Big things depend on little things. A little screw out of place in the locomotive can wreck the whole train. Big things depend on *little things being well done.* Let us remember that if ours is some little, humble task, it takes just the same grace and power as does the big thing our neighbor is doing. And the Master doesn't measure bigness of task, but the faithfulness of each one in the part asked of him.

Wednesday. Ps. 122:1-9.

HOW WORTHY GOD IS!

Worship is really thinking in the heart how worthy God is, how loving and lovable and how thoughtful of us. We can be doing this all the time, everywhere. But there's special blessing when we gather together with others to pour out our praise and worship, and to learn more of our wondrous God. He delights to have us do it. It is sweet to have fellowship with others in the things that we prize most.

Thursday. 1 Cor. 12:4-11.

FITTING INTO THE CHIEF'S PLAN.

The Holy Spirit's control in the life—this is the essential of the true life. He uses what he finds. And under his touch the natural gift is not only at its best, and helps others, but it fits in with all others in his broad, outreaching plan. Whatever the gift, the Holy Spirit's control is the thing, the one thing, that counts. Then one is *content with the task appointed,* however humble, since we know it is his wish.

Friday. Eph. 4:1-7.

GOOD WALKING.

We really cannot be worthy of our calling. No one can be worthy of the shed blood of the Son of God. But by his grace, we can *walk* worthily. What he asks us to do he gives us the grace to do. And like him, we are not here to criticize, but unitedly and singly to be ready and eager to join with our brethren in his service. To walk worthily is to walk as Jesus walked.

Saturday. Eph. 4:11-16.

HEARING —DOING—GROWING.

The full-grown man is the one who has taken in and made a part of himself the things that go to build up a man. One grows by the process of assimilation. We hear the truth. God has his appointed ones to build us up by teaching. But many remain babes in Christ, or very little children, because *obedience* does not follow the teaching. Jesus, forgive us: help us to *do* as well as to *hear.*

Thirty-Fourth Week

Sunday.   Luke 12:1-12.

PUTTING JESUS' POWER TO THE TEST.

Confessing Christ is not merely the form of standing or speaking in the presence of men for him. That is but a beginning. Confessing him is proving him able to save and keep in the day-by-day circumstances of one's life. No confession that stops short of revealing his power in the life is adequate. What does *your* life confess him to be? Lord Jesus, help us confess by thy power in our lives what a Saviour thou art.

Monday.   Acts 1:1-8.

THE LIFE SPEAKS THROUGH THE LIPS.

We cannot witness to what we do not know. If we are to witness for Christ, we must first let him in, and all the way in, and in control. Then we know his power, and are able to witness to it by word and by life. Words are powerful or weak, according to *the life back of them*. The privilege of knowing him personally and of letting the life bear witness of his power is great joy.

Tuesday.   Jas. 3:1-8.

A CONTROLLED TONGUE.

How grateful we are for the tongues that have brought the message of the Christ! So much of blessing comes through the tongue. But what hurt that little thing can do, also! Is it not strange that the tongue that brings some message of cheer and hope can also spit out words of reviling and evil? Then the good is clean rubbed out. The tongue must be *under control at its roots* down in the heart—the Spirit's control.

Wednesday.   Jas. 3:9-18.

"MUST" SPELLED BIG.

There's such a plenty of world wisdom. Perhaps that is the reason there is so much confusion today. We need the wisdom that comes from Jesus himself. It is blessed that Jesus says we may have it for the asking. And when we ask, he won't remind us of how stupidly unwise we are. He will give us his wisdom with the giving of himself to dwell and live in us. But he must be given habitual control—with that "must" spelled big.

Thursday.   Matt. 25:34-40.

HOPELESSLY BANKRUPT.

When someone does a kindness to our loved one in need, does it not stir the heart's gratitude as if it were done to ourselves? Ah, it is sweeter because we love our dear one so. Jesus loves. No one is beyond his brooding, wooing love. He is asking us to help all those in need. We're hopelessly in debt to him for what he has done; and *our debt is payable to all whom we touch.*

Friday.   Ps. 145:1-12.

GOD IS COUNTING ON US.

God is counting on us to tell his mighty acts. He counts on our getting in touch with himself, and experiencing his power to save, and to meet our every need. He counts on us telling others of him. This is his plan for reaching the others. There are mighty acts of loving-kindness that he wants to do. But he needs human channels. He wants to reach through us to the crowd. We limit him if we fail him.

Saturday.   1 Thess. 5:12-22.

INTERDEPENDENT.

We all need each other. We all need help. And we each can give help to someone. Our Master is expecting us to help, each the other. Sometimes we're ignorant of our need. Sometimes we're not ignorant, but too proud to admit the need and accept the help. When we do not feel the need, then the need is greatest. Whether we give help or receive it, let's be patient and gentle with each other.

Thirty-Fifth Week

Sunday.   Luke 6:30-38.

THE STANDARD OF GIVING.

The Jew was taxed a tenth. He gave it because he *must.* The Christian is supposed to *give as Jesus gave.* He held all subject to our need. We are to reckon that all we have is his. Then we're to give as his Spirit guides. Knowing about the world's needs, feeling its emergency, we're to hold everything subject to the Spirit's control, and habitually, t bought fully administer what we have, giving as he guides.

Monday.   Luke 20:45-21:4.

GIVING TO GET.

The world looks on the outside. Jesus looks on the heart. The world gives to get; *the average of the giving is to get.* The devil gives only to deceive and get a tighter hold. God gives to help only, regardless of thanks or appreciation. We're to be like him. Our giving is to be from the heart, and to the heart. Not putting gay patches on our clothes to attract attention, but quiet giving to help somebody.

Tuesday.   2 Car. 9:6-15.

A GIVING BALANCE.

Most of us have to work for bed and bread. Our waking hours are necessarily absorbed in getting. A few have a great abundance, and give lavishly. Yet the thing to mark keenly is *how the balance strikes between giving and receiving.* The man who gives much may strike a *getting* average. The main stream turns selfishly in. The man who has little may strike a *giving* balance. The main stream turns blessedly out.

Wednesday.   1 Chron. 29:1-5.

THE LIFE INCLUDES THE GOLD.

Money is needed, and it means much to give money. Lives are needed, too, and needed immensely more. It means yet more, aye, it means most, to give the life. And when the life is given, given not in a crisis, but slowly, faithfully through the long years, that means that the savings are given, too. We're to give our lives to Jesus, and for him, and then our earnings, too, as he guides.

Thursday.   Exod. 35:20-29.

THE RED TINGE.

It's the red mark of the life upon a gift that tells its worth. Here comes a poor man with some goat's hair. He comes shyly up and slips quickly away. Here comes a man with several big pieces of gold and puts them on top, and walks away slowly, so folks can see. And the unseen Eye looking says, "This poor man gave most, for the red tinge of sacrifice is on the gift." It's the gift like the Master's that does the Master's work.

Friday. 2 Cor. 8:7-15.

THE GIVING SPIRIT.

Liberality gets into a pretty high class here. It's a grace, like love and faith and patience and gentleness. It's a matter, not of purse and dollar marks, but of spirit and heart and touch with God. The poorest man in dollars may be liberal. The man whose giving takes six figures to tell may be close and stingy. It's all a matter of the giving spirit, that is, the Jesus spirit, in the heart.

Saturday. 1 Tim. 6:9-19.

SANE ON MONEY.

Some men own their money; some are owned by it. This is as true of little as of much. You can shut out the whole world with one small copper cent held close enough to the eye. As owner it sucks all the juices out of the heart; when owned and controlled it's the nearest to omnipotence of any tangible thing. It takes much of the Jesus spirit to keep a man sane on money.

Thirty-Sixth Week

Sunday. 1 Kings 21:11-20.

DON'T WOBBLE.

There's a fight on between evil and good. It's a desperate fight. Evil has the advantage of not being hampered in choice of weapons. Good has the better advantage of better weapons and of the sure outcome. Evil may conquer for a time. Good will win in the end, and meanwhile, too, if we're true. Jesus *is* victor, through his blood; and we shall be as we are true to him. But *there must be no wobbly compromise.*

Monday. Eph. 5:6-14.

ALWAYS CARRY THE LIGHT.

The Christian can go anywhere, as the Holy Spirit leads, but only for the purpose of carrying the light, either directly or indirectly. Wherever the light is carried, it overcomes the darkness. *Darkness can't stand the light.* Try it with a match in a dark room. It stays only where the light does not shine. When the Light of the world—Jesus—is allowed to shine out through us. the darkness of evil is always overcome.

Tuesday. Eph. 5:15-21.

CORNERING THE MARKET.

We must be keenly on the lookout for every opportunity to put in a bit of word or work that will count for Jesus, and so against evil. And *when there is no opportunity, make one,* persistently, boldly, but always tactfully. "Redeeming the time" is literally "cornering the market." That is, get in before the devil, and get hold and don't let go. Our Lord Jesus has redeemed all things. In his Name we take what he has bought.

Wednesday. Rom. 12:21-13:10.

EVIL CAN'T STAND LOVE.

The Christ spirit is the overcoming spirit. And the Christ spirit in control always means evil overcome. Indifference to evil strengthens it. Evil for evil intensifies the evil. Good for evil cuts at the very foundations of evil, and so not only overcomes, but undercuts it. Evil cannot progress where it meets the love spirit. It is only as love controls that one can hold steady. Love—pure, steady, winsome, aggressive, undiscourageable—evil can't stand that.

Thursday.   Dan.1:8-20.

DON'T SELL YOUR BIRTHRIGHT.

So much hinges on a single thing. Daniel was given a keen, understanding mind. He knew that he could keep it so or lose it. So knowing, he chose to be *careful in his habits of life*. "Pulse" for Daniel meant thoughtful moderation, self-control, which must have characterized all his round of life. Dainties may seem a small item, but Daniel would not sell his birthright of keenness and strength for a mess of dainties.

Friday.   Ps. 139:19-24.

THE SEARCHLIGHT.

When we're willing for God to search our hearts, then we have made a big start toward the only way that will prove lasting. Were you ever surprised at your failure under stress? But God was not. He knew the state of your heart would keep you from meeting that test victoriously. Lord Jesus, search my heart, and *lead me out of my own failing way* into thy way, the way of right, of victory.

Saturday.   1 Cor. 9:19-27.

THREE ALL'S.

There were *three "all's" in Paul's working creed.* He aimed passionately to let "all" of Christ into his own life. He aimed strictly and keenly to keep out of his life "all" that would grieve the heart of Christ. And then he aimed graciously, thoughtfully, even sacrificially, to be "all" things necessary in winning men. The "all" of taking from Christ; the "all" of giving to Christ; and the "all" of winning others for Christ.

Thirty-Seventh Week

Sunday.   Matt. 5:10-16.

SALTLESS SALT.

Salt keeps things from smelling had and from being bad. It preserves. It works unseen. You know of its presence or absence by smell and taste. Light preserves, too, and makes the way plain. Neither of them ever talks about what it's doing. It just *does.* That's its nature. We're to be *salt* and *light* to the crowd we touch through the Jesus life in us. And the crowd's quick to recognize saltless salt and rayless light.

Monday.   Acts 16:6-15.

THE TOUCHSTONE OF POWER.

There are calls for help on every hand. But as we keep quiet, with our heart absolutely willing to follow the Holy Spirit's leading, we shall know with certainty which "Come over and help" is the Master's call, to be followed. He knows the needs. There is a "Lord of the harvest." Except we fit into his plan, we really tangle and hinder, instead of helping. Not service but *obedience is the touchstone of power.*

Tuesday.   Neh. 1:1-11.

A PROGRAM-PRAYER.

Nehemiah's great heart bled for his people. Above everything else he wanted them to turn to God. His prayer gives a good program. He realizes sorely the result of disobedience to God; and his heart mourns over it. Then he realizes gratefully the gracious promise of God to those returning to the pathway of obedience. Then he pleads God's resistless power, as he presses on with the plan that has been shaping itself in his heart.

Wednesday.   Phil. 2:5-16.

A STRAIGHT ROAD.

When the Jesus spirit is allowed to control us, then the mind or disposition that was in him will be found in us. We are told what he was like. We are asked to be like him. There is just the one way to do it—yielding thoughtfully, intelligently, strongly, to the Spirit's gracious control. Then the daily quiet corner with the Book, the inner ear trained to hear, the outer life held true—these lead to Christlikeness.

Thursday.   John 4:4-15.

THE ETERNAL QUALITY OF LIFE.

Are you a "well" Christian, or a "spring" Christian? The woman said "this *well.*" She was thinking of a hole and a bucket and a lot of work to get the water up. Jesus really said *"spring,"* that is, a living, bubbling fountain that couldn't be held down or back. It's better to be a "well" Christian than none at all. It's best to let Jesus be the living spring within, ever bubbling up with *the eternal quality of life.*

Friday.   John 4:28-42.

THE REALEST WAY OF HELPING.

The woman found Jesus. She yielded to him. She was changed. She was so changed that people believed him just by seeing the change in her. That is *the realest way of helping people* know Jesus. Indeed, it is *the* way. No amount of preaching reveals Jesus to others, unless back of the words and in them there is that subtle, fragrant Jesus-touch that cannot be defined and cannot be resisted.

Saturday.   Rom. 10:8-15.

WAITING FOR US.

It is a great responsibility to know Jesus. We are responsible to the throngs who need his saving power. God *waits on us* to carry the message of Jesus. And the crowds wait. They would believe Jesus if only they knew him. We can tell those who are near; and we can help send somebody to the far-away ones. Let us know him intimately; then we shall take him fully and passionately to the others.

Thirty-Eighth Week

Sunday.   Matt. 25:14-30.

FRUIT CULTURE.

The vine doesn't try to bear grapes: it can't help it. It drinks in dew and rain and air, eats up soil food, basks in sunlight, yields without a flinch to pruning knife, and to re-straining cord, and to the acid spraying of the gardener. *Then the grapes come;* they must; they can't help coming. If we'll be as natural as the vine, and as sensible, we'll bear grapes too. And the whole process is in that word "abide."

Monday.   Matt. 5:3-10.

TRUE AND FAITHFUL.

We are not responsible for fruits in life, nor for results in service; only for keeping true in life and faithful in service—true and faithful to Him. Then he'll flood the "blesseds" in thick and fast. We're to practice *walking on our knees,* keep a sharp appetite for his food, yield to the pruning knife in his hand, and never get out of the dew and sunlight of his presence. He attends to fruits and results.

Tuesday. Ps. 1:1-6.

CHOCK-FULL.

You can't grow strong on "nots," but you won't grow strong without them. The presence of evil makes you line up and leave some things out. The best way to get and keep them out is to *fill the life chock-full of the positives.* Chew the cud of the Book. Keep your roots deep in the living waters. Breathe the wholesome air of His presence. There'll be no room for anything that oughtn't to be there.

Wednesday. John 16:22-28.

REFRESHMENT IN DRY PLACES.

Joy is distinctly a Christian word and a Christian thing. It's the reverse of happiness. Happiness is the result of what happens of an agreeable sort. Joy has its springs deep down, inside. And *that spring never runs dry,* no matter what happens. Only Jesus gives that joy. He had joy, singing its music within, even under the shadow of the Cross. It's an unknown word and thing except as he has sway within.

Thursday. Phil. 4:4-9.

GOD WITHIN, MAKING MUSIC.

Peace is a heart word. It's more. It's a heart thing. And the thing's immensely more than the word. The experience is so much more than can be told. And the heart controls life and mood and service. Peace is *God himself within making music,* holding off all storm and disturbance and discord. He comes in through the only door to the heart, the door of our glad consent to his unstinted presence and control.

Friday. John 15:1-8.

SCANTY?

A spring storm broke a large limb of a cherry tree. It hung by a slender connection. But the blossoms came, and soon the fruit began to grow as on the other branches. By and by the fruit ripened on broken branch and on unbroken. I didn't understand till one day Jesus' word "much" made me notice that only those branches in full connection bore "much" fruit, the broken branch "scanty" fruit. *How are your connections?* The fruit tells, much or scanty.

Saturday. 2 Tim. 4:1-8.

FINEST FRUIT.

We shall be like Jesus some glad day when we come up into his presence. We'll be like him in purity and goodness and in being wholly, thoroughly right. *This is the finest fruit,* the crown of the fruitage. It's the final fruitage in us, of his blood shed, of our choice of him persisted in, and of the gracious work within us of his Spirit. And each passing day may help ripen to the full that wondrous fruit.

Thirty-Ninth Week

Sunday. 1 John 3:1-8.

THE LOVE OF LOVE.

The Father's love is the real beginning of the Christian life. That love was so real that it gave the Only Begotten to make a way back for us to the old home. He never forces anyone. He wants our free choice freely given. That's *the love of his love for us.* But he does kindle the subtle, soft-burning fires of his love until we are mellowed and melted, and want to come back.

Monday. 2 Cor. 5:14-19.

FRESH FUEL.

When we feel the fires of the Father's love burning, then we start. The music of his voice catches and thrills, and we answer back. His love draws out our answering love. We open the door. He comes in and kindles his fires on the hearthstone of our heart. Then we put fresh fuel on the fires daily: studying his Word, chewing the cud of it daily, obeying it habitually—*this is the fresh fuel.*

Tuesday. Ps. 119:9-16.

THE EAR IN PRAYER.

God talks in the old Book. He talks out of the Book to us. Then we want to talk with him. Bible study is the listening side of prayer. He draws out our praise and love. He encourages us to ask definitely and expect confidently. Then we do as he asks. And *then he can do as we ask.* Obedience is keeping the door open to God. And he uses every door that is open.

Wednesday. Ps. 119:97-105.

THE SHORT ROAD.

Eating, breathing, sleeping, exercising—this is the common road to bodily health and vigor. Food, air, rest, activity—this is the road to Christian growth and vigor: the food of the Word well chewed; the fresh air of the Holy Spirit breathed habitually; the rest of trusting God confidently, unquestioningly, in tight corners and everywhere else; the lending a warm, helping hand unstintingly to others. It's an old road, and *it leads straight to the goal.*

Thursday. Eph. 3:14-19.

THE FAMILY FIRESIDE.

The Church is God's family. It's a school to learn and teach in, a hospital to get well in, a home to rest in—mind and body and spirit. It's a workshop to be busy in, doing the needful things. Above all, it's the Father's house, where the members of the family gather and look up into his face and bring grateful tokens of their love. All God's children should delight in *helping the family life.*

Friday. Acts 20:22-24, 32-35.

KEEP THE OUTLET CLEAR.

An outlet is as necessary as an inlet, and it must be in proportion to the inlet. When the outlet clogs, the inlet clogs too, and the waters get foul and gather bad scum. No outlet means a dead sea. Some lives are the coastline of a dead sea: the streams all flow in; the outlet's clogged; the waters can't nourish life. *Love gives.* That's its life. God gives. That's his life. Let's be like him. Clear away what stops the outflow.

Saturday. 1 John 3:16-24.

LEAKS.

If the pipe has good connections with the reservoir and with your house, you can get all the sweet fresh water that you want, and the pipe's kept clean inside, too. If we'll keep in close connection with our reservoir, the Lord Jesus, and with the house of life. our fellowmen—*no leaks at either end*—we shall know the sweet results in our own lives, and others will know of the blessed Master's presence.

Fortieth Week

Sunday.   Gen. 12 1-9.

IS YOUR LIFE SAVED TOO?

The call was clear. Abram had no doubt about it. It wasn't an easy call to follow. He could have stayed where he was and worshiped the true God in the midst of idolatries. That would have been a good thing to do in itself. But it wasn't the God-thing. His soul would have been saved, but his life lost, his opportunity gone, and gone forever. *Is your life being saved?* or only your soul?

Monday.   Gen. 17:1-8.

CHOOSING GOD'S CHOICE.

God has his plan for each life. He needs us in his plan for the world. He asks for the use of our lives. He proposes a working agreement. It's something quite apart from salvation. It's the use of our lives in his great purpose in the earth. And the one condition that he requires is that we follow fully, not only in our choice of right, but in *our choice of his plans.*

Tuesday.   Acts 7:1-8.

THE ONE UNFAILING THING.

The one unfailing quantity in life, and the only one, is—what? Banks fail, even with the Government guarantee back of them. Investments prove utterly unprofitable sometimes. Friends? Yes, they fail too, for lack of strength when not for lack of love. By the time a man gets the figure four at the beginning of his age, he finds that every thing and everyone has failed sometime, with the rare exceptions that prove the truth of the statement. *But God, Jesus—never yet.*

Wednesday.   Heb. 11:1-10.

THE TIPTOE OF EXPECTANCY.

Faith is being sure about the thing you hope for. Hope is more than desire; it is expectancy. The inner eye looks out and sees the thing in actual possession or realization before it really is. And so the life is held true to God. In spite of depression or of opposition one holds steady and quiet and true and keeps sweet. And the thing comes. *God never fails.* The fruits come, big and juicy.

Thursday.   Mark 10:35-45.

THE GREATEST GREATNESS.

The way up is down. True greatness is not in position nor in possessions nor in achieve-ments, but in what one is in himself when he's alone in the dark. To feed a hungry man in sore need, who doesn't appreciate your help, even when it means suffering and sacrifice for you—this is the real Christ-spirit. To be like Jesus himself in heart and spirit and action—this is *the greatest greatness.*

Friday.   Acts 13:1-13.

FITTING INTO THE PLAN.

There's a throne above the world. There's a Man on the throne. He has a plan for things down here during this time of turmoil and storm. His Spirit is down here to get that plan done. He needs each one of us. He puts his hand on each Christian life and says. "Separate yourself from all else for the bit I need you to do." His hand is on you. Are you doing it? *Anything else classes as failure.*

Saturday.   Isa. 41:8-16.

LINKED WITH GOD.

The exquisiteness of *doing* the Father's great, tender, wise, practical will—nothing, absolutely nothing, compares with that. Then there's God's own peace in the heart; the inner sense of his approval. Nothing can take the place of that nor compensate for its absence. There's the fragrant power in life and service, even while thorns tear. There's the wondrous joy of having a part with him in his wondrous world-plan. This was the blessedness of Jesus' earth-life, and may be ours.

ﬀortp-ﬀirst ﬁeek

Sunday.   Gen. 13:5-11; 14:14-16.

THE HURTING POINT.

The heart that responds to God always responds to another's need *to the hurting point,* if need be. There's a helping others that has little, if any, of the God-spirit in it. It's the thing to do; others do it; it's popular. The touchstone of the real thing is the willingness to do when it costs or hurts. It cost Abraham to help Lot. It cost Jesus to be our Saviour. It will cost to be a real Jesus-helper to others.

Monday.   Gen. 13:12-18.

BAD BARGAINING.

Bargaining is selfish, even bargaining with God. Jacob bargained with God. Jacob's kinsfolk seem quite numerous. The real Christ-spirit yields all to the Father because it's his, and trusts him to be a Father, *without bargaining.* The real Jesus-spirit in a man helps another because he's needy. Then there comes an unbargained-for double reward: we are like God, and we open the way for him to be God in full to us and through us.

Tuesday.   Gen. 18:16-23.

A STUDY IN MATHEMATICS.

Co-operation increases efficiency in amazing proportion. Two working together in perfect agreement have fivefold the efficiency of the same two working separately. The old Book says that where one can handle a thousand, two can dispose of ten thousand. This is as true in prayer as in action. A united Church would be an unconquerable Church. But the moment co-operation sacrifices an essential, real power is at the disappearing point. *First true though alone; then co-operation.*

Wednesday.   Gen. 18:23-33.

A TRAINED EAR.

Prayer is Spirit-suggested. It needs a strongly bended will. Through that comes the open or trained ear. So we learn God's plans. We catch the prayer he needs to have prayed. His promise turns into a prayer on our lips, and so it is a prophecy of what he will do. Thus prayer is restrained as well as inspired. Its whole purpose is to get God's love-will done through the needed human channels. *Prayer's touchstone is a trained ear.*

Thursday.   Rom. 12:9-21.

OTHERS!

What flows in must get an outlet or stagnate. God gives; it is his very life. Jesus served; it was the God instinct in him. The real God-spirit within must serve others. Not for return, nor for advantage of any sort; not for appreciation, nor thanks, but in the absence of these, even when misunderstood and criticized, it must serve, with exquisite tact, for *their sake only.* This is the characteristic of God and of true service.

Friday.   Matt. 15:1-9.

FREE SLAVES.

We owe everything, humanly, to our parents. Our life comes from them. They are fellow-creators with God of human life. And the months and years of care and devotion and forethought of us make us their slaves, *love's free, volunteer slaves,* forever. It is a constant parable to us of our relation to God. And the true child-heart will be utterly devoted to parents regardless of difficulties. It's the normal, healthful thing.

Saturday.   1 Tim. 5:1-8.

GUARDING THE IDEAL.

Home is love's abiding-place. It may be palace or cabin or neither. It isn't brick and timber, though these may hold most fragrant memories. It's a school to learn in, a resting-place from toil for spirit and body, a shelter from storm, an atmosphere where the heart qualities come to richest fruitage. An ideal? Yes. Let studious restraint be on everything that would mar that ideal, and earnest cultivation be given everything that would make it real.

ᚠorty-Second Week

Sunday.   Gen. 21:1-12.

GOD'S MORE.

God's delays are love-planned. So the gold is refined, and more is given and got. Abraham waited long for Isaac. And the waiting made a new Abraham, and so the son was a wholly different, finer man because of the new father. Abraham had all he longed for, and more; that "all" became choicer, higher grade. And God had more to use, and the world-plan in his heart was saved thus far. *God's delays are love-inspired.*

Monday.   Gen. 22:1-14.

ACTUALLY PERFECT.

God is ideal, intensely practically idealistic. He insists on the gold being wholly pure, the will wholly strong, the heart wholly perfect in its devotion, the life wholly right. Nothing less will do, even though it cost his own Son's life to bring things up to standard. And he leads the way in showing us the way. His taking from us is *never to make us have less.* Following his way, we *have* more and we *are* more.

Tuesday.   Gen. 15:4-6; 22:15-19.

KEEP THE DOOR OPEN.

God *could* give to Abraham, because he had made such a wide opening into his life. God can give only into an open hand. This hand was opened wide. This door swung clear back. God had a free swing, and he used it. He *could,* and he did. He always does. Let this be our rule: *"Give all he asks; then take all he gives."* And the cup will be spilling joyously over at the brim.

Wednesday.   Matt. 10:37-42.

AND THE CROWD'S LISTENING.

Love does its best, and gives its best, and is its best. That's a fixed law. That's the law of love. That's *the love of love.* And so you always know how much there is by how much is given and done and been. Love can't help itself. It must. That's its life. Otherwise it shrinks up and gasps and dies. How much do you know of love? It's easy to find out. You're telling daily.

Thursday.   1 Sam. 1:9-18.

BIGGER PRAYING.

Hannah's praying changed. Hannah herself changed. She wanted a son; that was all. Then in God's gentle love-fire her vision cleared and broadened, her will mellowed and bent. She was willing that God might have her son in his sweeping plan for a nation. So she became more. So she got more than a son, a national leader, and through him a world-Saviour. *God would change the gauge of our praying* so he can enlarge the gauge of his giving.

Friday.   1 Sam. 1:19-28.

MORE.

We can give God more by letting him have *more of ourselves*. Hannah could give God more now. She had more. She was more. Samuel was more than she had dreamed of at first. He became the man he came to be by the spirit of the woman that brought him. So God's world-plan of a Saviour-nation, and through it the world-Saviour, was saved. Hannah gave more in her son because she had given more of herself.

Saturday.   Luke 14:25-35.

RED FOOTPRINTS.

Sin makes sacrifice. It grows pain. There were no thorns in God's Eden. Because of sin things are wrong in the world. And so we are called upon to put out every selfish thing and *leave out some things not selfish*—that God may have the freest use of us in his plan for a world. So Abraham gave up the dearest thing to him, his son, and Hannah her's, and so much more, God his.

Forty-Third Week

Sunday.   Gen. 24:57-67.

HOLD STEADY.

Mating-time is life's sweetest time thus far, and life's most serious. A slip there is the most serious of all mistakes. God's plan for his saviour-nation hinged on Isaac's getting the right helpmate. So he plans each life, and each union of lives. So he'll bring his Isaac to each Rebekah, and his Rebekah to each Isaac. But we must hold true to our ideals, and to him, and *keep steady during the waiting-time.*

Monday.   Gen. 2:18-24.

THE GATE INTO THE NEW EDEN.

The true unit of society is not a man or a woman, but a man *and* a woman joined in heart by the touch of God's own hand. Each fits into and complements the other. There's a chosen Adam awaiting every Eve, and a choice Eve being prepared for each Adam. But only God's fatherly hand can bring them together, and knit them into one. This is where *God's hand should have fullest control* if there's to be a new Eden for each two.

51

Tuesday.   Eph. 5:22-33.

THE STRONGEST KNOT.

Leadership and co-operation are absolutely essential in action. Man has been given the duty of leadership in the action of life; woman co-operation with him in his leadership and responsibility. They are bound together by the strongest of ties—love. There should be no rivalry nor competition, but the constant fellowship of strong, thoughtful, matured and maturing, restraining, and sacrificial love. *Only love makes strong life.* So each does the best and is the best and gives the best.

Wednesday.   1 Cor. 7:10-17.

THE HUMAN HOLY OF HOLIES.

Nowhere is it so essential that God be given full place, and his own plan full sway as in the sweetest and most serious of all relationships—that between husband and wife, the holy of holies of human life. He makes us fellow-creators with himself in life's most sacred relationship. We should be controlled here, never by mere sense of pleasure, but *only by the same strong purpose that controls his creative power.*

Thursday.   Matt. 19:3-9.

EQUAL TO ANY EMERGENCY.

Sin has broken God's Eden plan of marriage. And a bad break it is, too. Sexual conditions are always an index to general moral condition throughout history and around the world. And divorce is an unfailing index finger to general sexual conditions. Christ's plain teaching was clearly against any breaking of the marriage tie. God's grace and power, with prayer and patience, are *equal to any situation or emergency,* however difficult. So only can there be victory in the life.

Friday.   John 4:5-19.

A RARE BLEND.

Jesus was so true. Gently, with exquisite tactfulness, but definitely, clearly, he put his linger down on the sore spot in this woman's life, and held it there until she shrank under that firm touch; yet with such friendly humanness of touch that her life was radically changed. It was *an exquisite blend of truth and grace,* with the victory that that blend always brings. That was rare courage in its scarcity as well as in its preciousness.

Saturday.   Prov. 31:10-31.

LIFE'S HELPMATE.

God's greatest gift to man is woman. In the simple Genesis story she was taken out of man's side that she might *always be at his side,* inspiring, helping, strengthening; his companion in all his problems and difficulties and joys; teaching him what love is by being love itself to him, and so drawing out the best of love and of all his powers. But God's hand *must be strong in the life* if his wondrous plan is to be real.

Forty-Fourth Week

Sunday.   Gen. 25:27-34.

RARE SELF-MASTERY.

Sin teeters things over, out of poise. Its fever steals away self-control; simple, strong trust in God under every circumstance holds us steady and content. Selfish longing for material advantage beyond his fair share led Jacob to tempt his brother. Bodily hunger, uncontrolled, made Esau underrate a sacred trust. Both lost control. Both had bad diseases, very contagious; epidemic still, everywhere. Poise—*rarest of all rare things*—comes through Jesus' control strong in the life.

Monday.   Rom. 14:13-23.

WHEN IN DOUBT, DON'T

If a thing's doubtful it isn't doubtful for the man who would ring true. If there's a question mark on a habit or a custom or anything, that should rule it out instanter. The thing may be wrong, then the case is clear. It may not be wrong; but it may, possibly. Then it belongs out. No one cares to eat a doubtful egg. *When in doubt, don't* is the only safe rule for him who would be true at any cost.

Tuesday.   1 Cor. 8:1-13.

TRUE GENTLEFOLK.

A gentleman will never do as he properly may if it will hurt someone else. For gentleness is strength accommodating its strength to someone weaker. Gentleness in its first meaning is manliness. And manliness will be true to itself in dealing with another, and never take an unfair advantage. Jesus was the truest of gentle men. *Gentleness is love in contact with others.* It gladly puts a restraint upon itself for the sake of another.

Wednesday.   1 Cor. 10:23-33.

DUTY STANDS SENTINEL.

Duty is what is due to oneself or to others. If I drink an intoxicant it may hurt my acquaintance who is struggling bravely against a fevered appetite. It is my duty not to. So I won't, even though I might. It will injure my own body, loosen my control upon my will power, make me open to other evil habits, dull my judgment. My duty to myself calls for restraint. So I won't. Duty sternly forbids.

Thursday.   Heb. 12:14-17.

WISE CHASTISEMENT.

Chastisement doesn't mean an actual whip, though with some it may include it, when they haven't strength enough, or love enough, for the higher, better level. It means instruction, information, training, that a man can see where he is wrong. But it means more, doing it so lovingly, tactfully, patiently, that he not only knows he's been wrong, but he wants to do right; and, more yet, he makes a start that way.

Friday.   Num. 11:4-13.

POOR MEMORIES.

Appetite, uncontrolled, makes a man lose his good sense. These people had better noses than memories. They could smell the leeks and onions and melons, but they forgot God! Their stomachs were dominant. They preferred using their teeth to using their thinking powers. The truck gardens of Egypt are recalled, but not the taskmasters, the bricks without straw, nor the wondrous gateway out of Egypt. They seem to be kin to some of us.

Saturday.   Ps. 78:29-40.

BLACK DISOBEDIENCE.

Disobedience is never commonly dubbed as bad and as black as it really is. Under any veneering, cultured or coarse, it is *devilish*. The core of the devil's spirit is to set one's own preference up against God's. When one remembers that God is more tender than a mother, more eagerly devoted than a lover, and more sensitive to pain and slight than any human, the black badness of disobedience begins to stand out in all its ugliness.

Sunday.   Gen. 27:18-29.

DELAYING GOD.
Selfishness delays God's love-plans. There is no more unpromising character in the Old Testament than Jacob. Back of unscrupulous bargaining and unprincipled trickery was intensest selfishness. Why did God use him? As Abraham's grandson he was one of the only two that could be used in the world-plan being worked out. He was the least unusable of the two. And he had to be changed before the plan could work out. He delayed God. Selfishness always does.

Monday.   Gen. 27:1-10.

CHOICE PLUS GRACE.
Which is more in making character, heredity or training? the influences before birth or those after? Before birth parents should thoughtfully emphasize a planned heredity. Afterward it should be recognized that training can overcome any heredity. Poor Jacob was handicapped both ways on his mother's side. Bad handicap that! Yet—yet, listen, a determined will *and* God's resistless, gracious power can overcome any handicap.

Tuesday.   Gen. 27:11-17.

IMPULSE OR PURPOSE?
A man's character is revealed most by his sober second thought. An impulse may be bad or good; a deliberate purpose is worse or better; it can strengthen or check the impulse. Esau was impulsive, a bundle of impulses, sometimes good, sometimes weak or bad. God couldn't use him. Jacob was the stronger character, a cool, deliberate thinker. That made his badness worse, and his goodness better, when at last he yielded his life to God.

Wednesday.   Gen. 27:30-45.

MOTIVE MORE THAN EMOTION.
Weak impulses or bad ones, yielded to, are hard on the tear-ducts. There's bound to be a bad emotional storm before the thing's over. Tears are very impressive; they sway a lot of people. But one should look through the tear-mist to see what motive controls. Motive is more than emotion. If Esau had been thoughtfully right in his motives beforehand, his emotions wouldn't be having such a hard time now.

Thursday.   Gen. 37:29-36.

PAYING THE BILLS.
Sin is self-executive. Every sin pays its own bills. There's a hell of suffering in every sin. When sin is let into the life its brood—pain, broken hearts, broken lives, remorse, and worse—comes in, too, and *some day will break out* and run riot, unless a stronger power intervenes. Jesus' dying is appreciated fully only where sin's badness is fully recognized.

Friday.   Acts 5:1-11.

THE CORE.
Of all deceptions religious deception is the meanest, the most contemptibly irreligious. In pretense there's a veneering of the purest and holiest of all things—devotion to God. It's supposed to be that way clear into the core. It really covers up the unholiest and impurest of things—selfishness. But it doesn't hide them long. The veneering's too transparent, as a rule. Nobody's befooled; least of all God. *Let's be the same at skin and core,* pure and true.

Saturday.   Eph. 4:20-32.

CLEAN WINDOWS.

The rose uses neither paint nor perfume. It's just itself. That is the touch of its Maker. Truth is transparent. The window glass is clear. The whole house is open to inspection. That's the touch of God. The Jesus-man needs neither paint nor perfume of profession or good deeds. He needs only to be made and kept clean by the blood of Jesus; then *to live clean and true* in the simple round of his daily life.

Forty-Sixth Week

Sunday.   Gen. 28:10-22.

GOD WINS.

God and sin are sharp rivals: sin, ugly, hard, persistent, and God relentlessly pure, gently, patiently wooing men. It's a continual nip and tuck, with God a head and a heart in the lead. The sting and hurt of sin are everywhere. And God is always on the heels of sin to heal the hurt, neutralize the sting, and woo the man. Jacob flees from Esau's hounding hate. God eagerly pursues Jacob. *And God wins.*

Monday.   Gen. 27:46-28:9.

STUPIDITY AND WOOING.

God's wooing never ceases while there's the least chance of winning. Isaac's blessing—in the very language used—was a reminder to scheming Jacob that only through God's blessing *could* he be blest or succeed. His cunning bargaining would fail. Its results wouldn't be worthwhile when the final reckoning was made. They would only embitter his last years. He goes stupidly on scheming and bargaining, depending on himself alone, but the wooing goes on, too, and finally wins.

Tuesday.   Gen. 29:1-20.

THE LIFE LOST.

It's rank folly ever to get *out of God's plan* for one's life. One's soul may be saved, but his life is lost, and his future next-world seriously affected. When a man insists on his own plan regardless of God's, the lines tangle, the thorns grow thick, the moral sense dulls. He may pray, but as he insists on his own way, there will be weary toiling and a bitter tang. Jacob knew this with a bitter, biting certainty.

Wednesday.   Exod. 2:11-22.

GOD'S INSURANCE.

Going God's way is an insurance policy against accident and violence and death, until one's life-errand is full done. Doing any other way opens the door to all sorts of danger. Ask the unnamed prophet in 1 Kings 13. A man never need run from danger when doing what he should. Ask the three young men in Daniel 3. The protecting presence of the "Fourth" is unfailing in the path of obedience.

Thursday.   Jonah 1:1-17.

NINEVEH OR TARSHISH?

Every man of us is either in the caravan to Nineveh or on the boat to Tarshish; headed due east, or just the reverse, due west; going God's way or his own. Which way are *you* headed? Some of us go to Tarshish *religiously.* We sing and pray while going our own way and straight across the grain of God's way for us. Are you traveling by land or water? to

Nineveh or Tarshish? God's way or your own?

Friday.   Ps. 139:1-12.
THE MOTHERLY GOD.
Can a wee baby of the tender weeks get away from the mother? No more can we get away from the loving, brooding presence of God. His unfailing love keeps in unbroken touch. Our very sitting down, our getting up—who would bother about such details of one's common, everyday life? Nobody but a mother, or— *God*. His strong, warm hand is always close down over us. Let's not try to get away, but to live in touch.

Saturday.   Ps. 139:14-24.
THE GENESIS PLEDGE.
God gave himself *to* us in Eden and at our birth, his breath, creatively. He gave himself *for* us on Calvary, his blood, redemptively. He gives himself *with* us continually, his Spirit, sustaining, wooing us if we keep him out; shaping the life over on the shape of his own presence as we let him fully in. John 3:16 is written on the first pa.ges of Genesis. In giving his breath he pledged his blood if ever the need came.

Forty-Seventh Week

Sunday.   Gen. 33:1-11.
WINNING BY BENDING.
Pray, and do your best, and then pray some more, and things will come out right. But "pray" means a strong will bent to the higher will. Jacob's exquisite tact and studious preparation *coupled with dependence on God* won Esau's heart. But it was a new Jacob now, broken-legged and bent-willed, weakened in his own human strength. God could help now. His strength was being made perfect in action through a bended human will.

Monday.   Gen. 32:3-12.
PUSH UP THE CALENDAR.
Sin breeds fear. Perfect love makes fear turn tail and flee. If we could be freed of all sense of fear, we'd have new bodies, the physician's calling would be largely gone; we'd have keener minds, saner judgment. and better-balanced lives. Some day Jesus, in actual control, will *turn fear out-of-doors to freeze* in the winter blast. And that "some day" may be pushed nearer on our calendars than most of us think.

Tuesday.   Gen. 32:13-23.
EXPENSIVE SELFISHNESS.
Selfishness is expensive. Sin comes high. It costs time, strength, heartache, and bitter tears. Jacob was terribly frightened when he was willing to part with all that valuable livestock, the choicest he had, representing long years of sweat and skill and sleepless nights. That was the rarest wealth to him. It was for just such wealth he had cheated and deceived and lied. Sin's charges are terribly high. Selfishness is awfully expensive. Better stop before you start.

Wednesday.   Gen. 32:24-32.
A CHANGED STEP.
No; he didn't. The "Man" wrestled with Jacob. It says so. Jacob *clung* to the "Man."

56

Jacob was thinking about the terrible danger. But God was thinking about Jacob and the world-Plan that centered in him. Jacob was so stubborn. God had to change his step before he would walk God's way. Jacob's stubbornness made the case desperate, exceptional. Then weakened Jacob, awake at last, *clung* in desperation. And God *could* bless him.

Thursday. Matt. 18:15-22.

DON'T!

Unwise criticism is the commonest and most hurtful thing in life, next to sin. Its acid touch burns and blights everywhere. Jesus gives us here the simple love-law of criticism; this: Never criticize anyone, with four qualifications: (1) except to *help;* (2) then *alone* with the person concerned; (3) then only from your *knees* and on your *knees;* and (4) in the spirit of utmost *humility* and persistent *forgiving love.* When that fails personal responsibility ends. But—"love never faileth."

Friday. Matt. 18:23-35.

THE SPONGED-OFF SLATE.

Ten million dollars off the slate at one swipe of the sponge! That *would* be some forgiveness. That's Jesus' picture of God. The man with the sponged-off slate putting a brother-man in jail for sixteen dollars and sixty-odd cents! That's Jesus' picture of some men. How small sin can shrivel us up! But how *can* you forgive? Jesus' love in the heart will make you love the one you can't like.

Saturday. Luke 6:27-38.

BURN 'EM!

The only decent way to get rid of one's personal enemies is to—not kill them with knife or bullet or social frost, but to *burn 'em up.* But only one kind of fire will do it, the fire of love, God's own love, that burns you *out* while it burns him *up;* all the bitterness in your heart goes *out,* melting into tenderness, and all the enmity in him goes up, consumed in regret and sorrow.

Forty-Eighth Week

Sunday. Gen. 37:18-28.

THE ONE ANTIDOTE.

What a horrid brood it is, this serpent's ugly brood of hate—envy, jealousy, bitterness, lying, heartlessness, cruelty, slavery, if need be, murder; the milk of human brotherliness and filial affection curdled thick and sour with the sharp acid of hell; vipers poisonous brooded of vipers venomous! Horrible! the only safe thing is to strangle the smallest beginning before it gets born. And the only antidote is love, *but the real thing,* God's own love in us.

Monday. Gen. 37:1-8.

BE TRUE.

Goodness arouses the bad in those that are bad. A piece of red-hot iron plunged into cold water makes a lively disturbance. A true Christian, living a true, consistent life, lovingly, in the common round of life, will arouse antagonisms. Jesus' mere presence in the world stirred up the greatest demon activity on record. *The* thing is to keep strongly, steadily on being true and pure and gentle, in spite of opposition, and avoid extremes.

Tuesday.   Gen. 37: 9-17.

SENSITIVE GODWARD.

Dreams and visions are pretty much relegated to a dreamy, visionary, unpractical realm with us Western Hemisphere people, and quite rightly, as a rule. Yet there may be, with the earnest, thoughtful Christian, the cultivation of *a sane, quiet sensitiveness of spirit toward God* which enables us to discern ahead in spirit how things should go, and how they will turn out, and what decisions should be made. It is God's touch guiding and helping us keep true.

Wednesday.   Col. 3:18—4:1.

THE BIG THING.

The love spirit lives *true* wherever it is, and whatever the relationship. We should be rightly eager to make the most of life's opportunities, but whether one is slave or master, employee or employer, in hidden away corner or in the limelight, *the thing that matters most* is this: being true and pure just where we are, and, with this, being patiently, gently, thoughtfully loving in all personal contacts. So Jesus did, and so we should and may.

Thursday.   Ps. 105:1-22.

GOD IS DEPENDABLE.

"Providence" means that God *sees ahead* how things are going, and that he *sees to it* that nothing will hurt his trusting, obedient child. Jesus' one concern in the Wilderness wasn't about starving, but to keep true. The Father would attend to the bread in good time, even if he had to send angels. If we *see to it* that we obey faithfully and intelligently, God will *see to it* that all comes out well.

Friday.   Eph. 6:1-9.

"HONOR THY—."

Humanly the child owes everything to the parents. They are fellow-creators with God. From them comes all the child has of life and vigor and distinctive talent. And so it is due the parents that the child give the heart's love, the life's obedience, and the faithful devotion of years. And this given will adjust the relation between the children. The only exception is where an instructed conscience forbids obedience to some requirement.

Saturday.   1 Corinthians 13.

IT NEVER FAILS.

Love never fails. It cannot; for it is love. It's not a sentiment merely, but a passion. It feels keenly, thinks deeply, plans intelligently, waits steadily, believes in the outcome without the shadow of a doubt. It gives, gives its very self, gives till the blood comes, and then till it quits coming because it's all gone; but it never fails. It never fails in devotion, in intelligence, in patience, in suffering, nor in results. *God* is love.

Forty-Ninth Week

Sunday.   Gen. 41:33-44.

THE TIME-TEST.

God never forgets, and never fails. *Waiting is the acid test of strength.* The turn in the long road comes at last. It had been a long road for Joseph. It had been a desperately rough road, too. There was the slimy pit, the brothers' treachery, the slave chains, the terrible palace temptation, and the prison cell. But strength believes God. It bides *his* time. It trusts in the darkest hour. And God never fails and never forgets.

Monday. Gen. 41:1-13.

KEEP IN TOUCH.
God is practical, so intensely practical. He can be depended on, absolutely, in every blind alley, for every sort of help needed. If a man'll quietly, strongly keep in simple, full touch of heart and *head* and *life* with God, he'll become equal to any emergency that comes. Wisdom, dollars, strength to hold true, gift of leadership, whatever is needed, will come, and it will come in time. *The thing* is to keep-in touch and hold steady.

Tuesday. Gen. 41:14-24.

OPEN UPWARD.
God prefers using natural ways of working out his plans. Nature is really his method of working. He speaks to Pharaoh through a dream, so vivid that it seems distinctly significant. He makes clear to Joseph's mental processes just what that significance is. Joseph is *open to God.* So he could *get* what was being *given.* Keep open to God in heart and *head* and *life;* and when you need rain look toward the sea.

Wednesday. Gen. 41:25-32.

GOD'S CLOCK.
There's a simplicity about God in working out his plans, yet a resourcefulness equal to any difficulty, and an unswerving faithfulness to his trusting child, and an unforgetting steadiness in holding to his purpose. Through a fellow-prisoner, then a dream, he lifts Joseph from a prison to a premiership. And the length of stay in the prison prevents dizziness in the premier. It's safe to trust God's methods, and to go by his clock.

Thursday. Matt. 25:14-30.

SCHOOLTIME.
This is schooltime. We're in training. There's a new order of things coming to the earth some day. God carries an ideal in his heart. Some day he will carry it out on this old earth. In that ideal time coming he will need men and women whom he has trained, and whose experience and judgment he can trust. *Let's be good scholars in school,* patient, steady, quick to learn, with unfailing trust in the Teacher.

Friday. Luke 19:11-27.

THE BLUE RIBBON.
Faithfulness rates highest in God's school. We have different abilities and gifts. Some can do things that others can't, and some can do things better than others can. But the highest marks in God's school at examination time are not given to ability but to *faithfulness.* Faithfulness doesn't mean being full of faith. It means that God can have faith in you that you'll be true to him—persistently, consistently true to him.

Saturday. Neh. 5:1-13.

LIVE IT!
Truth is best preached by being lived. Nehemiah *was* what he required. The best binding for the Bible is shoe leather. For thirty years Jesus only *lived,* just lived a simple, every-day life, *lived all he* taught those few after-years, and lived more than he could teach. A man embodying the truth of Jesus in his daily round is worth more than libraries of sermons, invaluable as these may be. *Let's live it,* for Jesus' sake.

Fiftieth Week

Sunday.   Gen. 45:1-15.

WISE FORGIVENESS.

Wise forgiveness is difficult and rare. It needs an exquisite blend of graciousness and firmness. Joseph had a ticklish job on his hands. His brothers didn't want forgiveness. They weren't penitent. It wasn't simply that he should have a forgiving spirit toward them, but that he should so handle them as to lead to that brokenness of heart in them that would long for forgiveness and be grateful for it, and become utterly changed in conduct.

Monday.   Gen. 43:15-25.

IT TAKES BRAINS.

To forgive in your heart is often a pretty tough task. It's a fight with yourself. It's a matter of your heart and will. Yet it is the easier part of forgiveness, even when not easy. To *tell* your forgiveness, and *make the other eager for it*—ah! that's another thing, a far harder thing. That's a matter of brains and tact. It's the heart stimulating the gray matter of the brain. Yet this is what forgiveness means, often.

Tuesday.   Gen. 43:26-34.

RARE DIPLOMACY.

Never was diplomacy—love's wooing, winning diplomacy—sent on a harder mission than when Joseph set out to do—what? Be willing to forgive his brothers' terrible conduct toward himself? No, no; something far different: to make them really broken-hearted to think they should have treated him so. This explains all his rarely keen, subtly shrewd—yet always loving and honest—handling of them, from first to last. This sets the standard for real, full forgiveness.

Wednesday.   Gen. 44:1-13.

A PICTURE OF GOD.

Joseph is a wonderfully vivid picture of Jesus, and so of God. He was misunderstood, envied, hated bitterly, plotted against even to the point of death. His brothers were hardened in their attitude to the last degree. His task of love was to handle them so tactfully and wisely and firmly that his love would change their hearts toward him, and so their character. It's a wondrous picture of God's forgiveness. And God's is the standard for ours.

Thursday.   Matt. 6:5-15.

LOVE. IN REAL CONTRAST.

Close contact intensifies personal feeling, both hate and love. It's harder to forgive your near kinsman than someone you never saw. Family feuds are always the bitterest. King George and Emperor William are cousins. The terrible war was a family fight. Does this explain its bitterness, partly? Yet we're all brothers, blood brothers. We're all sons of the one Father, creatively. Love that's really love *controls all of one's contacts.*

Friday.   Col. 3:5-17.

INTO THE CORE.

Ah! now we're digging down to the underpinning. The forgiving *spirit!* That touches the inner core of the thing. Not things *not done,* not words spoken merely, nor even kindly acts done, but the *breath* that penetrates one's being like an atmosphere, and sends a perfume, intangible but real, and as fragrant as wild roses, into the nostrils of the other one. That *is* forgiveness. That is *God.* That is *human,* the real human.

THE OTHER FELLOW.
The other fellow has something to forgive, too. Don't let's forget that. He has our un-forgiving spirit to forgive, at the least. And what is harder to come up against than that? Or, what is harder to forgive? And then there's God. What has he to forgive in me and you? The only place where you are sure, really sure, not to fall is flat on your face in the dust, pleading God's forgiving grace.

Fifty-First Week

A FINE TEST.
It's an ugly thing to see a young man, trained in the finer conventionalities, ashamed of the old-fashioned folks from the old country home. It's a bad sign. There's something wrong. Joseph's kinsfolk were foreigners, their occupation utterly despised, their manner of life wholly strange to the Egyptians. It would have been easy for some to have been ashamed of them. But not this ruggedly true Joseph. *Loving loyalty to father and mother* is a fine test of character.

THE HOME-FOLKS.
Joseph looked after the home-folks. He did it thoughtfully and graciously. They must share the prosperity that had come to him. It's one of the fine touches. It reveals his wholesome goodness. *Prosperity is one of the acid tests* of character. It is so often hard on the old home-ties. It loosens them. It's bad when success dulls old home loyalty. The heart should be true to God and self and to one's kin.

BE CAREFUL OF THE SEED.
Great things happen through simple circumstances. A simple thing this: a family migrating from one country to another, a very common thing. But what a great thing! Here come the "makings" of *the* nation through which came the world's Saviour and future King. They're coming to the land and the difficult experiences that will transform a tribe into the world's most remarkable nation. And all because Joseph held true. *Let's hold true, regardless, yet lovingly.*

NEEDS REPRINTING.
The family is the controlling unit of life in the Orient. There the family tie is the strong-est of all ties. Here in the Western Hemisphere individual initiative—everyone free to swing out for himself—is the controlling characteristic. Both Orient and Occident go to not-good extremes in this. A wholesome blend of both is the normal thing. We need to strengthen' wholesomely our family loyalties. The Fifth Commandment needs reprinting with big type in American life.

THE BEST KINDLING.
Joseph was a good fireman. He was an expert in the right sort of kindling. He might have used other handy kindling, some called "righteous wrath" and "holy retribution."

There was the temptation to, without much doubt. But love was in control clear through. He used kindling and *coals of love.* He used them freely, heaped them up; the fire grew hot. So he mellowed and melted the hearts of his brothers. Wanted: more firemen of this sort.

Friday.   Luke 15:18-24.

LISTEN!

Some of us need to go back home. We're in church perhaps, active in Sunday-school maybe, busily tied up doing good things possibly, giving pretty freely it may be, all absorbed with religious things and patriotic likely, but—but we need to go back home. The Father wants to talk with us a bit. He has something to say, and we need to hear it. Let's sit down quietly, unhurriedly, and listen to the Father's voice.

Saturday.   Ruth 2:18-23.

IS RUTH IN YOUR BIBLE?

Like a lonely flower, fragrant in the midst of weedy growth, is this little story of Ruth; like a gleam of clear shining in the dark, stumbly night; like sweet love, tender and pure and true, flanked by hating and fighting and intrigue. We're needing more Ruths in *the Bible of daily life;* more being true and pure and fragrantly, wholesomely loving in the commonplace rounds and relationships. It's the finest telling of the God-story, the gospel.

Fiftp-Second Week

Sunday.   Isa. 9:2-7.

GOD WILL DO IT.

Every promise of God's is a prophecy of what he means to do, and what he surely will do. Sin may delay but cannot prevent God's plans working out. In one of the darkest hours of Israel's story, and the world's, there shines out boldly, clearly, in striking contrast with the gloom all around, this exquisite promise of what God meant to do for the world. So our dark hour shall know bright gleams of light *if we'll keep our face Godward.*

Monday.   Luke 2:1-7.

THE NEW CENTER OF GRAVITY.

The promise has become a person. Prophecy has taken human form. The old pages are full of someone coming. In these newer leaves he has come, actually come. With all the humanness of a mother's expectancy become a thrilling experience, of a father's protecting care, of a babe's wondrous face and presence, aye, of cramped quarters and a world busily, noisily hurrying by unnoticing, unappreciative, *He* has come who yet will be *the world's center of spirit gravity.*

Tuesday.   Luke 2:8-20.

THE DECISIVE TEST.

It was the thing to do, what these shepherds did—go to see for themselves. The personal test is the decisive test. It *is* the thing: go to Jesus direct and find out for yourself. Of course, they hadn't far to go. Neither have we. Get into a quiet corner, with the door shut, and the Book open, the knees and will bent, and *you'll* find out for yourself the reality of Jesus for your life and your problems.

Wednesday. Luke 2:25-35.

CAN YOU SING?

Simeon had been taking vocal lessons and practicing for a long time. He had the Master-musician for his teacher—the Holy Spirit. His ear was trained by careful listening. Expert listening is really skilled silence. He had caught the true keynote and could sing it, and sing it accurately, without flatting or sharping or sliding, hitting every note clear and true. We need more singing of this sort. And *the singing-school is still open.*

Thursday. Matt. 2:1-12.

THE RESISTLESS MAGNET.

What drawing power Jesus had, and *has!* Away from the Far East he drew these thoughtful men, on a long, tedious journey, through strange lands, without any guidebooks, but with the unerring starry guide. And he hasn't changed. He still draws men, from East and West and every other point of the mariner's compass, and from every point and angle of the compass of need and difficulty. *Let's hold Jesus up.* Men'll come to him. They can't help it.

Friday. Luke 3:39-52.

BLESSED COMMONPLACE.

What is there uncommon about those Nazareth years? Just this: they weren't un-common. Jesus lived the simple, common life of the average man of all the race, so far as outer circumstance goes. This was the Father's plan. So he came into closest sympathy with all men. And so he put the in-tensest emphasis on *living* as the chiefest thing in life, just living, true and pure and gentle, in the common round, and in the Father's recognized presence.

Saturday. John 1:1-5.

GOD WITH US—IMMANUEL.

In the beginning there was a Wondrous One. He was the mind of God thinking God's thoughts out to man. He was the heart of God throbbing love out to man's heart. He was the voice of God talking music into man's ear. He was the face of God looking into man's eyes, that we might be caught with the beauty of his face, and come running back home. He was God himself bearing a human name—Jesus. *And he is with us.*